50
1962-
2012

Fiftieth

Anniversary

Edition

The fourth printing of this book is dedicated to
Grand Master Ansei Ueshiro, honoring the 50th anniversary
of his arrival in the United States,
for the express purpose of bringing Shorin-ryu Karate-do
to these shores.

SHORIN-RYU

*Okinawan
Karate
Question and Answer
Book*

SHORIN-RYU
Okinawan Karate
Question and
Answer Book

Meditation while in the seiza position. It takes years to develop mushin, the ability to clear the mind of all thoughts.

TITLE PAGE: *Superimposed on the Shorin-ryu seal is Master Ueshiro performing a flying side kick (yoko tobi geri).*

Okinawan Karate Question and Answer Book

by

William Cummins
Robert Scaglione

Illustrations and Diagrams by
William and Maureen Cummins
Typography by Rob Smith

PERSON-TO-PERSON PUBLISHING, INC. New York

For Grand Master Ansei Ueshiro
Fourth Edition 2010

Credits: Grateful acknowledgement by the authors is made to Yoshinori Maeda for sharing his invaluable knowledge of Shorin-ryu philosophy, Jeff Brooks, editorial. Mei Chow, calligraphy, Lynne Holmes, typing, Terry Maccarone, encouragement, Michael Mackay, photography, Emiliano Mazlen, Edit Revision, 2010, Paul Maluccio, Update and revisions.

Distributed by Shorin-Ryu Karate USA
shorinryu.com

Published by Person-to-Person Publishing, Inc.
© Copyright 1984 by Robert Scaglione and William Cummins
Printed in USA
First Edition, 1985
Second Edition, 1991
Third Edition, 2002
Fourth Edition, 2010
ISBN 0-8048-1426-0

Contents

History   *13*

Kata   *23*

Kumite and Weapons   *35*

Karate   *47*

Japanese Terminology   *57*

Appendix   *69*

The kio-tsuke (attention) position. The fingers are lightly touching the gi and are positioned slightly to the front. They touch each other and the thumb without tension. The body is relaxed with the eyes fixed straight ahead.

Introduction

It is a privilege for us to share our thoughts on karate here with you. It is our intention to answer some of the many questions we have been asked over the years in order to inform and perhaps to enlighten you, and in so doing to help perpetuate the art of karate.

We approach this task with the greatest respect and admiration for those who came before us: the masters, the sensei, the karateka, the deshi and all the practitioners of karate-do. It is through them that we have learned this way of life; it is due to their devotion to their art that we may carry on its traditions.

We present our thoughts to you with humility, with the sense that whether we have practiced karate for ten or twenty or fifty years we are and will remain deshi, students. The practice of karate is never completed.

* * *

Karate is a unique art. Although there are many fighting methods in practice around the world they differ from karate technically, philosophically and in practical application. Despite some superficial resemblences karate is not the same as judo, boxing, kick-boxing, tae-kwon-do, savate, sumo, kung-fu or any other martial art.

Karate developed in the Ryukyu Islands over the last several hundred years. The Okinawan bushi (warriors) were often under circumstances in which weapons were not available. They were required to face armed opponents empty handed. It was to meet this challenge that karate was developed.

"Karate" may be translated as meaning "empty hand." The characters may also be read as "China hand." This reflects one source from which karate was made.

Okinawa, the main island in the Ryukyu chain, is located midway between Japan and China. For centuries

The bow (rei). From the kio-tsuke position the body bends forward at the waist with the eyes, neck and shoulders moving together as one. The fingertips lightly graze the gi as the body moves. The bow should not be made too low. Fundamental to Shorin-ryu is the observance by practitioners of courtesy and mutual respect.

Calligraphy: Martial path.

it served as a convenient stop over for ships traveling between those two nations. Okinawa's strategic location made it a place where these cultures could cross-pollinate; a uniquely fertile ground where the best of both worlds could grow.

* * *

Before the early 1960's only a handful of westerners were acquainted with karate. In 1962 Master Ansei Ueshiro came to the U.S. expressly to bring the once secret art to a wider public. It is due to Master Ueshiro's unceasing devotion to karate-do that we are able to make our contribution.

The philosophical foundation of Shorin-ryu karate is built upon the philosophy of Ankichi Arakaki, uncle of Master Ueshiro. Arakaki Sensei, more than anyone else, influenced the inner attitude and outer practice of Master Nagamine, a most important Sensei of Master Ueshiro.

Master Ueshiro is of the bushi (samurai or warrior) class by blood. His first teacher, as was often the case in Okinawa, was his father. But even as a child he began to study with some of the venerated masters of his time. Although these men worked as farmers and fishermen they were the true masters of the art of karate.

They recognized extraordinary qualities in their young student: his phenomenal physical strength as well as his perseverance, his devotion to his family's art and his fine mental character.

Master Ueshiro was trusted and appreciated by these masters who trained him, and soon he was training with the top karateka in the world. Just a few years later he was part of a group of karateka without equal, a group who lived the true warrior tradition. Among its members were Sensei Taba, Sensei Kina and Sensei Shima.

Master Ueshiro has been immersed in the warrior tradition of karate all his life, through his uncle, his family, and through the various dojo where he practiced. It is essential to recognize that these traditions and philosophical and spiritual precepts, taught and handed down from sensei to sensei, are as much a part of Okinawan Shorin-ryu as are the kata and techniques.

* * *

In the 1930s, 40s and 50s there were some in Okinawa who sacrificed everything – their jobs, families, social

"What is life for, if not to dance!"
ZORBA THE GREEK

"The art of archery is not an athletic ability mastered more or less through primarily practice, but rather a skill with its origin in mental exercise and with its object consisting in mentally hitting the mark. Therefore, the archer is basically aiming for himself. Through this, perhaps, he will succeed in hitting the target – his essential self."
HERRIGAL

"In oneself lies the whole world and if you know how to look and learn, then the door is there and the key is in your hand. Nobody on earth can give you either the key or the door to open, except yourself."
KRISHNAMURTI

position – to dedicate themselves solely to the practice of karate. These sensei would practice from morning till night, everyday, continuously.

Master Ueshiro, as he matured and had a family, found it necessary to place karate second to giving his family financial support, something that was not possible through karate or the dojo.

I would emphasize that in the modern western world it is most important to be employed, self-sufficient, productive, and to seek to be successful in life for oneself and family. Karate should come second to the goals of success, family and education. It is the objective of karate in the philosophy of the Shorin-ryu system, that karate be a vehicle towards achieving career success outside the dojo, as well as harmony with one's family and friends. The spirit of karate must be applied through hard work, diligent effort, physical and mental stamina, thereby motivating one to success in his or her goals. This success should not and must not be sacrified because of karate training but rather karate should compliment one's spirit and character. The manifestation of any challenge besetting the karateka must be met and conquered, whether the challenge be a physical confrontation, a stressful job, a psychological situation or an unattainable goal. Once presented, all challenges will be swiftly dealt with through one's spirit, strength and character. This is the objective and reward of dedication to karate. This is Master Ueshiro's philosophy. This is our philosophy. This is our Shorin-ryu system.

*   *   *

The art of karate, like that of architecture or music, is something that has been created by the efforts of thousands of people over the course of centuries.

The truth inherent in karate has been made manifest by countless hours of practice, innumerable repetitions of kata and techniques, throughout decades and entire lifetimes.

There is no shortcut to perfection. There may be those who think that they know all there is to know because they have practiced the outer forms of the art and had a glimpse of something beyond. But this kind of finality is a mirage. They are only deceiving themselves. There is always more work to be done.

Again, there are no shortcuts to perfection in the study of karate. To the dedicated student karate offers a vast wealth of knowledge and enlightenment. But it is only available through hard work and training; it comes as a direct result of the karateka's own effort, under the guidance of his or her sensei.

Each person who takes up the practice of karate receives the benefit of the experience of those who have gone before him. And each of us must deeply appreciate how far the art has been developed by their work. No one is born with the mastery of an art. Even a "genius" must study and practice for many years before he attains mastery. No novice could compose a symphony or design an aircraft without great labor first. A musician, an engineer or an architect each builds upon foundations laid by previous practitioners in their field. The same principle holds true in karate. We must humbly accept the enlightened teachings of the masters. Mixing the arts, confusing styles, dilutes and weakens those styles' original value.

There is an old saying "Many paths, one summit." Applied here we may see that two masters may have used very different methods to get to the same place; two very different ways of practicing which nevertheless lead the devoted student to a peak of ability. But two paths cannot be followed at once. This would lead to endless distraction, running back and forth between and never reaching the distant goal, the summit to which either road, followed with perseverence, would ultimately lead.

There are those who claim that they have no need for tradition. That they can do better on their own. They deceive their students and fool themselves. Dispensing with tradition is foolish and futile no matter how capable the practitioner may be.

It is as if, for example, an untrained person were to try to fly a 747. He may have great skills, talent, intelligence, but he does not have the right skills to accomplish the task. What should he do? Try to repeat decades of experimentation and practice? Or apprentice himself to an experienced teacher so as to be able to pick up where his predecessors work left off? The former is futile in aeronautics or karate. Only the second way holds the promise of success. By following the traditional path the skills that are required are already available.

* * *

In order to survive the art of karate needs you. Your desire to learn, to practice and to work at karate. And

"Be always displeased with what thou art, If thou desirest to attain to what thou art not; for where thou hast pleased thyself, there thous abidest. But if thou sayest I have enough, thou perishest. Always add, always walk, always proceed. Neither stand still, nor go back, nor deviate."

SAINT AUGUSTINE

10

further, karate needs your willingness to share your knowledge, to motivate others to practice karate. As we teach we learn.

We must have the spirit to strive for perfection in ourselves and to inspire and help others in their quest for perfection.

* * *

Karate is an art, a study and a practical application of an integrated philosphy. It embodies physical, emotional and spritual values which may be applied to all phases of one's everyday life.

To accomplish this there exists one simple vehicle. That vehicle is kata, the essence of karate. Kata embodies all the secrets, the mystery, the physical, mental, emotional and spiritual concepts of the masters. Kata is the key, the answer, the solution to everything that we search for in karate. Kata is zen. Kata is simple yet difficult. Like the wind, it is motion as in the physical performance, yet motionless. It is attainable yet unattainable. Once grasped it may slip away only to be grasped once again. It is a perfect imperfection. Kata is real yet a dream, a very possible dream. It shows our strength while making us aware of our weakness. It is a passive way to destroy and kill. It is brutal and vicious in a most humane way. Kata transforms destructive power into a flurry of beauty. "To teach kata is to learn kata," and from that maxim applied to life, an unbroken cultural chain is created and sustained. This is karate-do.

ROBERT SCAGLIONE
AUGUST 1982

History

The history of Shorin-ryu karate has for the most part been passed down over the years by word of mouth. As a result, contemporary writings have multiple spellings of the names of people and places as well as different dates of key events. In writing this book, we have used spellings and dates most commonly found in our exhaustive research and/or those that were handed down to us.

1   Name the major schools of Okinawan karate.

2   Name three teachers of Shoshin Nagamine.

3   When was Shorin-ryu karate founded?

4   Who founded it and where?

5   Who was Master Ueshiro's first sho-dan?

6   What year did Master Ueshiro arrive in this country?

7   What year was Master Ueshiro born and where?

8   Who first brought Shorin-ryu karate to the United States?

9   Approximately how many Shorin-ryu schools are presently operating in the United States?

10 Who was Master Ueshiro's second sho-dan?

11 What do the words Shorin-ryu mean in English?

12 What year was Okinawan karate introduced to Japan?

13 Who introduced it?

Ueshiro Sensei, grand-master of Shorin-ryu karate USA.

14 Who was the teacher of "Bushi" Matsumura?

15 Who was the teacher of Ankichi Arakaki?

16 of Chotoku Kyan?

17 of Choki Motobu?

18 In what year was the term karate officially agreed upon as the designation of empty-handed self-defense art and by whom?

19 What style of karate did Gichin Funakoshi originate?

20 What style of karate did Chojun Miyagi originate?

21 Why did karate develop in Okinawa when it did?

22 What rank does Shoshin Nagamine hold?

23 Who awarded him this rank?

A group picture taken in approximately 1957 shows from left to right, back row: Seigi Nakamura, Shiro Ikema, Shinei Kyan, Shoshin Nagamine, Jokei Kushi, Junko Yamaguchi. Front row: Masao Shima, Shoko Akagon, Ansei Ueshiro.

Yakusoku kumite san. Shihan Ansei Ueshiro, with Sensei James Wax, first American black belt, 1957.

24 What other titles does he hold?

25 What rank does Master Ueshiro hold?

26 What is Master Ueshiro famous for?

27 What technique was Ankichi Arakaki famous for?

28 What technique was Chotoku Kyan famous for?

29 Who was the teacher of Ansei Ueshiro?

30 What was Chotoku Kyan's main teaching?

31 What year was Shoshin Nagamine born and where?

32 Who originated the term Matsubayashi-ryu?

33 What does it refer to?

34 What is "Karate Sakugawa" famous for?

35 Who were some teachers of Gichin Funakoshi?

36 Give the year of birth and death and the age at death of the following masters; Ankichi Arakaki, Choki Motobu, and Chotoku Kyan.

37 Give the place of birth of the above masters.

38 What was Anko Itosu famous for?

39 What was the nickname of Choki Motobu?

40 Name the country of origin of the following martial arts: 1 arnis 2 bando 3 bandesh 4 bersilat 5 capoeira 6 hwarang-do 7 kendo 8 lua 9 pankration 10 pentjak-silat 11 savate 12 tai-chi-chuan.

41 Name the four major styles of Shorin-ryu karate in existence today.

42 Name the founders of each of those styles.

43 Name the two major groups of Okinawan karate.

44 What do the words Shorin-ryu mean in Chinese?

45 In what year did karate emerge from its veil of secrecy?

" *Karate-do is not merely a sport that teaches how to strike and kick; it is also a defense against illness and disease.*"

"*The correct understanding of karate and its proper use is karate-do. One who truly trains in this do and actually understands karate-do is never easily drawn into a fight.*"

"*There is no first attack in karate.*"

"*Karate is just like hot water. If you do not give heat constantly, it will again become cold water.*"

"*You may train for a long, long time, but if you merely move your hands and feet and jump up and down like a puppet, learning karate is not very different from learning to dance. You will never have reached the heart of the matter; you will have failed to grasp the quintessence of karate-do.*"

"*What you have been taught by listening to others' words you will forget quickly; what you have learned with your whole body you will remember for the rest of your life.*"

FUNAKOSHI

16

Ankichi Arakaki

Choki Motobu   Chotoku Kyan   Choshin Chibana   Kentsu Yabu   Chomo Hanashiro

1 Shorin-ryu, Goju-ryu, Uechi-ryu, Matsumura Orthodox, Isshin-ryu, Okinawan Kempo.

2 Ankichi Arakaki, Chotoku Kyan, Choki Motobu.

3 Approximately 1820.

4 "Bushi" Matsumura in Shuri.

5 James Wax.

6 September 14, 1962.

7 April 20, 1933. Kin, Okinawa.

8 James Wax opened the first Shorin-ryu dojo in the United States in Dayton, Ohio in 1960 upon instructions of his sensei, Ansei Ueshiro.

9 Hundreds-possibly thousands.

10 Robert Yarnall.

11 Young Forest style and or Pine Forest style.

12 1922.

13 Gichin Funakoshi.

14 Karate Sakugawa.

15 Chotoku Kyan.

16 "Bushi" Matsumura.

17 Kosaku Matsumora.

18 1936, Chojun Miyagi, Chomo Hanashiro, Choki Motobu, Chotoku Kyan.

19 Shotokan, from Shorin (Shuri).

20 Goju, from Naha.

21 In the 17th century Okinawa was occupied by Japan and a ban was placed on weapons. This ban forced the Okinawans to study Chinese boxing in secret for their own self defense. Gradually, out of this practice an indigenous

---

KUSANKU *China-18th century Chin military officer. chuan-fa (fist-way pra cioner. Arrived Okinawa in 1761. Deme strated techniques, but no kata.*

KARATE SAKUGAWA *(1733-1815) Shu Okinawa. Traveled to China many tir with Kusanku. Combined chuan-fa w tode forming "Okinawa-te" or "kara (China-hand.)*

SOKON 'BUSHI' MATSUMURA *(179 1882) Founder Shuri-te. Formulated seis naihanchi, ananku katas.*

YASUTSUNE 'ANKO' ITOSU *(1830-191 Shuri, Okinawa. Educator who was instr mental in introdecung karate to the O nawan public school system in 1901. Inve tor of the pinan katas.*

KENTSU YABU *(b. circa 1870) A sen student of Itosu. Became chief of kobayas ryu upon Itosu's death. Introduced karate Hawaii in 1927.*

CHOTOKU KYAN *(1870-1945) Shu Okinawa. Founder shobayashi branch Shorin-ryu. Passed down the passai, chir and kusanku katas.*

CHOKI MOTOBU *(1871-1944) Shu Okinawa. Considered the best fighter Okinawa of his time. Our yakusoku kum derive from Motobu.*

CHOSHIN CHIBANA *(1887-1969) Foun er, kobayashi branch of Shorin-ryu. Intr duced fukyugata ni kata into Shorin-ryu.*

ANKICHI ARAKAKI *(1899-1927) Shu Okinawa. Most important teacher of Nag mine. Matsubayashi philosophy of techniq and living based on teaching of Arakaki.*

SHOSHIN NAGAMINE *(1907-1997) Toma Okinawa. Founder of matsubayashi bran of Shorin-ryu. President of the All-Okinai Karate-do Association. 10th degree black be Composer of fukyugata ichi kata.*

ANSEI UESHIRO *(1933-2002) Kin, Okin wa. World Champion 1958-62, retired unco tested. Direct blood descendent of ancient Ok nawan "Bushi" class, one of the few such men the world today. Founder of Ueshiro Shorin-r Karate USA. Considered one of the best pra titioners of bo kata in the world. Composer fukyugata san kata.*

Shorin-ryu Genealogy

MATSUBAYASHI
(OKINAWA)

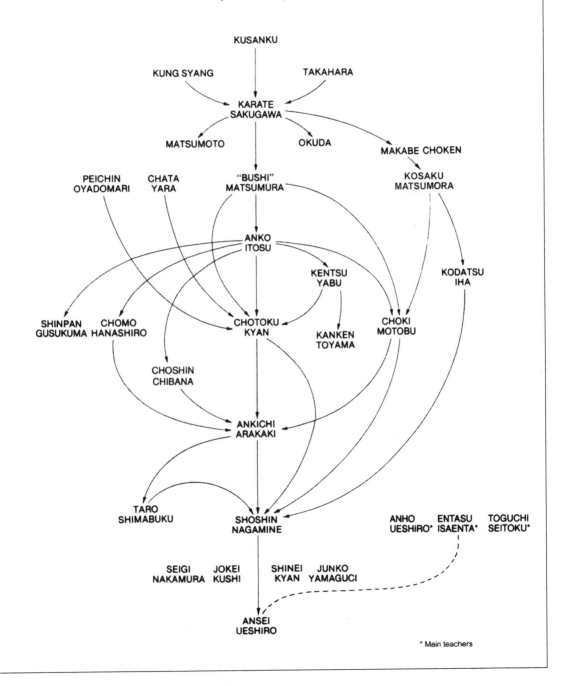

* Main teachers

style of fighting evolved which was the precursor of what we now know as karate.

22 Hanshi-sen, tenth dan, red belt.

23 The followers and sensei of matsubayashi karate-do. He is also president of the All Okinawa Karate Association.

24 Third Degree, kendo. First degree, judo.

25 Hanshi – Shorin-ryu Karate U.S.A.

26 He is considered by many to be foremost master of bojutsu. Also he was world champion for four years (1958-1962) and retired uncontested.

27 He introduced tsumasaki-geri (toe-tip kick) to the Shorin-ryu system.

28 Natural stance.

29 Anho Ueshiro, Entasu Isaenta, Toguchi Seitoku.

30 Never move back and develop one skill that fits your body.

31 1907, Tomari.

32 Shoshin Nagamine.

33 It is in honor of two outstanding karate men: "Bushi" Matsumura and Kosaku Matsumora.

34 He was a samurai who became the first known master of what is now called karate. He was also the composer of the Sakugawa bo kata.

35 Yasutsune Azato, Anko Itosu.

36 1899-1927, age 28. 1870-1945, age 75. 1871-1944, age 73.

37 All three were born in Shuri, Okinawa.

38 Inventor of the Pinan kata.

39 Motobu, the monkey.

Shoshin Nagamine

"To be ignorant of what happened before you were born is to be ever a child. For what is man's lifetime unless the memory of past events is woven with those of earlier times?" CICERO

"Karate is not a game. It is not a sport. It is not even a system of self-defense. Karate is half physical exercise and half spiritual. The karateist who has given the necessary years of exercise and meditation is a tranquil person. He is unafraid. He can be calm in a burning building." MASOYAMA

"Silence is the essential condition for happiness." UNKNOWN

"Time will be important to the man who has no patience. If he be waiting for a loved one, 10 minutes is a long time. If he be training for perfection, 50 years is just a beginning." WONG CHUNG-YON TEACHER OF YARA

"The only secret is to practice seriously and with perseverance, in order to attain the state of mushin which opens the doors of the hara to consciousness." MASTER EGAMI

"He who conquers himself is the greatest warrior." KARATE PRECEPT

"Karate is a lifetime marathon." NAGAMINE

40 1 Philippines 2 Burma 3 India 4 Malaya 5 Brazil 6 Korea 7 Japan 8 Hawaii 9 Greece 10 Indonesia 11 France 12 China

41 Kobayashi-ryu (young-forest style), shobayashi-ryu (small-forest style), matsubayashi-ryu (pine-forest style) and matsumura orthodox.

42 Choshin Chibana (Kobayashi-ryu), Chotoku Kyan (shobayashi-ryu), Shoshin Nagamine (matsubayashi-ryu) and Hohan Soken (matsumura orthodox).

43 Shorin-ryu (or Shuri-te) and Shorei-ryu (or Naha-te).

44 Shao-lin style.

45 In 1901, Anko Itosu introduced karate to the Okinawan public school system.

Some Thoughts About History

The history of karate is cloaked in mystery as is all history, with different dates, facts, reasons, names, times and places. This holds true especially in karate as it was only passed on by word of mouth and was not recorded because originally the practitioners were sworn to secrecy.

Consequently there are no known records, books or drawings from these early times. We cannot refer to documents but we must satisfy ourselves with the folk tales and myths of our predecessors.

The "truth" lies in the kata. The series of movements obviously developed with much thought and toil. The interpretations are also part of history and are as diversified as is any art.

The beauty and genius of these interpretations lie in the fact that we can still continue to learn from the techniques in the kata by exploring the movements, disecting them and using our own imagination which was the intention of the composers of the kata. The rest is history, the history of karate.

Kata

1 What is the definition of kata?

2 Name the five categories of basic movements.

3 How many kata in matsubayashi karate-do?

4 What are the naihanchi katas designed to develop?

5 In fukyugata ichi, which move is kiai?

6 How long does it take on the average to master one kata?

7 What is the longest and most difficult kata in Shorin-ryu?

8 What is the most important thing when practicing kata?

9 What is the most important thing when demonstrating kata?

10 What is occuring when one performs a kata perfectly?

11 Starting from attention and ending at attention, how many moves in fukyugata ichi?

12 Can you name all nineteen kata?

13 How many moves in each kata?

Kata naihanchi sho.

14 Who composed which kata?

15 When composed?

16 Which speed is best to practice kata?

17 What is the head's role in performing kata?

18 Is kata like bicycle riding, once learned never forgotten?

19 What is the role of the feet in kata?

20 When doing kata, how much tension should be in the body?

21 How many kata should we attempt to master throughout our karate career?

22 How many did the masters master?

23 Is it necessary to learn every kata?

24 Do the present day masters know every kata?

25 In karate, what is the single most important aspect?

26 Name the four basic principles in order of importance of body/mind as they apply to kata and everything else we do.

27 What is the most important kata in the system?

28 If only one kata is important, why do we learn so many?

29 What is the most important move in the kata?

30 What is the strongest or most powerful move in kata, the move which should neutralize your opponent?

31 What is the general rule for breathing in kata?

32 Once one perfects a kata, does it always stay with us?

33 What do the fukyugata, pinan and naihanchi kata teach us?

34 At what level does one begin to perfect kata techniques?

"A mastery of karate does not depend on the learner's physical constitution, but mainly on constant practice." KYAN

"When you practice karate, think of your arms and legs as swords." AZOTO

"There is no coming to consciousness without pain." CARL JUNG

"We need only one ingredient to operate at our full capacity. Pure unrefined joy." JACK SCHWARTZ

"Anyone can learn karate." ANSEI UESHIRO

1 Kata can be defined as an organized series of prearranged defensive and offensive movements symbolizing an imaginary fight against several opponents and performed in a geometical pattern.

2 The five categories of basic movements are: kamaekata (ready stances) dachikata (stances) semekata (attacking techniques) ukekata (blocking techniques) gerikata (kicking techniques).

3 Nineteen.

4 Strong legs and a strong kiba-dachi stance.

5 All moves in all kata are kiai.

6 Approximately three years or 3,000 to 10,000 repetitions.

7 Kusanku, consisting of sixty moves and requiring ten years to master.

8 At half speed the most important thing is concentrating on performing each movement correctly. At three-fourths speed, imagining an opponent is the important thing and at full power, focus would be the emphasis.

9 Showing power and focus.

10 There is endless speculation on this. One of these is that the kata exists externally and is brought to life by the (transient) performer. Conversly, when performing perfectly, one becomes the kata, thereby ceasing to exist as an individual ego.

11-15 See chart A, page 27.

16 The best way to practice kata would be to do many at half speed and then at the end of the practice session do some kata with snap and finish up with some full power kata.

17 The head should be used to lead the body around on all turning movements.

Master Ueshiro performing Chinto kata.

25

18 No, without constant practice ones kata deteriorates drastically.

19 Seeking and establishing the next position.

20 There should be no tension until the end of the technique at which time there would be one-hundred percent muscular contraction for a split second.

21 We learn many and perfect one. It would take a lifetime to perfect one or two kata and very few of us ever attain this goal but we strive for it like an impossible dream.

22 One.

23 No, it is necessary to learn the basic kata up to and including the naihanchi in order to develop oneself. After that one or two kata are enough.

24 No.

25 Kata.

26 1. Eyes (perceptions-sight-"mai").
   2. Balance (foundation-footwork-posture).
   3. Spirit (desire to do, win-heart).
   4. Strength (physical-power-breath).

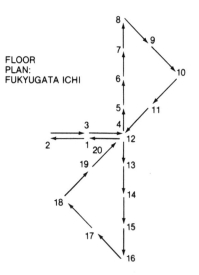

FLOOR PLAN: FUKYUGATA ICHI

"Failure is natural. We should never get disheartened by failure. Nobody has ever achieved anything great without failing. Ask yourself why you failed and learn something. Every failure must be a stepping-stone for your further success. Use all your failures as stepping-stones, one after another; then they are helpful experiences." SWAMI SATCHIDANANDA

"Life is movement and movement is life." B.K.S. IYENGAR

"Eating properly will not by itself keep well a person who does not exercise; for food and exercise, being opposite in effect, work together to produce health." HIPPOCRATES

"We shall not cease from exploration, and the end of all of our exploring, will be to arrive where we started, and know the place for the first time." T.S. ELIOT

"You can master an insane elephant; you can close the mouth of a bear or tiger; by alchemy you can earn your bread; you can wander incognito throughout the universe; make the gods your slaves and preserve eternal youth; you can walk on water and live in fire; but—to control your mind is better and more difficult." THAYUMANAVAR

"True art has no goal and no purpose." MASTER AWA

26

Shorin-ryu Kata

(MATSUBAYASHI)

KATA	COMPOSED OR INTRODUCED BY	BORN	BIRTH PLACE	WHEN COMPOSED	NUMBER OF MOVES
1 FUKYUGATA ICHI	SHOSHIN NAGAMINE	1907	TOMARI	1940	21
2 FUKYUGATA NIDAN	CHOSIN CHIBANA	1887	SHURI	1940	18
3 FUKYUGATA SANDAN	ANSEI UESHIRO	1933	KIN	1960	17
4 PINAN SHODAN	ANKO ITOSU	1830	SHURI	1907	22
5 PINAN NIDAN	ANKO ITOSU	1830	SHURI	1907	22
6 PINAN SANDAN	ANKO ITOSU	1830	SHURI	1907	16
7 PINAN YONDAN	ANKO ITOSU	1830	SHURI	1907	20
8 PINAN GODAN	ANKO ITOSU	1830	SHURI	1907	18
9 NAIHANCHI SHODAN	BUSHI MATSUMURA	1796	RYUKYU		19
10 NAIHANCHI NIDAN	BUSHI MATSUMURA	1796	RYUKYU		19
11 NAIHANCHI SANDAN	BUSHI MATSUMURA	1796	RYUKYU		13
12 ANANKU	BUSHI MATSUMURA	1796	RYUKYU		21
13 WANKAN					35
14 ROHAI					27
15 WANSHU	WANSHU		CHINA		33
16 PASSAI	KYAN	1870	SHURI		39
17 GOJUSHIHO	(AMMENDED ROYAL OKINAWAN FOLK DANCE)				54
18 CHINTO	CHINTO				43
19 KUSANKU	KUSANKU		CHINA		60

CHART A

27 Your kata, the one you are developing through years of training.

28 The fukyugata, pinan and naihanchi kata were developed to give us a foundation. Only with this foundation can we go on to learn and develop an advanced kata. The basic kata are a path or vehicle to the development we strive for all our life.

29 The move you are doing at the moment.

30 The move you are doing, each move is kiai even the yoi ready position.

31 Breathe in on blocks, breathe out on attacks.

32 No, only with constant training.

33 The fukyugata kata teach us the basic stances and techniques. They also introduce us to courtesy. The pinan kata teach us more advanced techniques. The naihanchi kata teach us kiba-dachi and foundation. Together these develop a deshi into a kareteka. Then one first begins to understand kata.

34 Yondan and above, although not in all cases. The rank does not make the man, the man makes the rank.

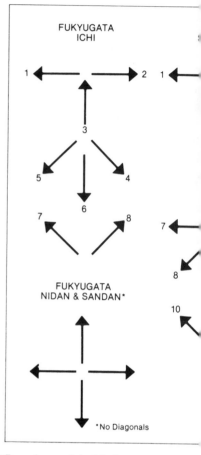

FUKYUGATA
ICHI

FUKYUGATA
NIDAN & SANDAN*

*No Diagonals

"*From the age of six, I had a mania for drawing the form of things. By the time I was fifty, I had published an infinity of designs, but all that I have produced before the age of seventy is not worth taking into account. At seventy-three I have learned a little of the structure of nature, of animals, plants, birds, fishes, and insects. In consequence, when I am eighty, I shall have made more progress; at ninety, I shall penetrate to the mystery of things; at a hundred, I shall have reached a marvelous stage; and when I am a hundred and ten, everything I do, be it but a dot or line, will be alive.*" HOKUSAI

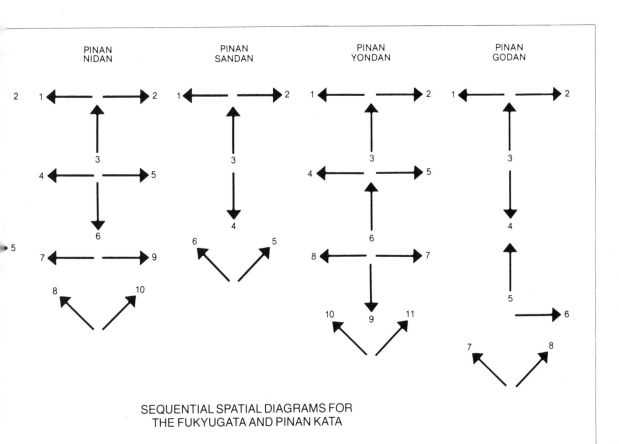

PINAN NIDAN   PINAN SANDAN   PINAN YONDAN   PINAN GODAN

SEQUENTIAL SPATIAL DIAGRAMS FOR
THE FUKYUGATA AND PINAN KATA

*"He who masters breathing can walk on
the sand without leaving footprints."*
               CHINESE SAYING

*"When merit has been achieved, do not
take it to yourself. If you do not take it to
yourself, it shall never be taken from you."*
               LAO TZU

*"There is one thing in art that is worth-
while. It is that which cannot be
explained."*   GEORGES BRAQUE

29

Interpretation and Significance
of Shorin-ryu Kata

FUKYUGATA KATA	Basic movements. Developing a foundation.
PINAN KATA	Peaceful. Developing flowing movements.
NAIHANCHI KATA	Horse riding. Concentration of strength inside the thighs. Developing a powerful stance. Fighting with back to the wall.
ANANKU	Chinese roots. A "basic" advanced kata.
WANKAN	King's crown. Advanced.
ROHAI	Light bird-like movements. Silent. Powerful as a swan, stork or heron.
WANSHU	Chinese roots. Hidden fist.
PASSAI	Breaking through or away as when one is ambushed.
GOJUSHIHO	Fifty-four steps. Royalty kata. Many subtle diversified movements.
CHINTO	Quiet, not boisterous. Serious fight to the death for recognition in a spiritual way. No spectators.
KUSANKU	Chinese roots. Most advanced kata.

Some Thoughts About Kata

Kata as explained in the text is the most important element of karate. Equally important is one's approach to utilizing kata as a vehicle to self-development. The sensei must insist on the display of patience in the deshi's attitude.

What may at first appear to be the longest road, in reality may be the quickest way to achieve a goal. The student who perfects kata correctly, one at a time, building a strong foundation, will excel.

We must not rush, greedily requesting to learn the next kata before we truly comprehend and are able to execute the techniques and movements of the kata at hand. The practice of only one kata, sometimes referred to as our favorite kata, is an important conclusion to reach. This kata is utilized to correct bad habits and to develop our skills. As we perfect one kata, we consequently perfect all of our kata because we become the movements. The true practitioner and kata cannot be separated.

The moves of a kata are easily learned but the real challenge is to allow the movement to flow. This is achieved by seeking perfection in the move or technique, emptying the mind as in a meditation, and allowing the move to happen. The kata then becomes a part of the karateka and the karateka becomes the kata. Only then can we move ahead. This is not measured in months or years but rather by the individual's performance.

Special exercise oyo-tan-ren

Master Ueshiro Demonstrates Kata Fukyugata San-dan

Attention, Bow, Ready 1,1A: Down-block and middle-punch, 2,2A: Two down-blocks stepping forward 3,3A: Double-punches 4,4A,4B: Down-block, high-block and middle punch (left-side) 5,5A,5B: Same on right side 6,6A,6B: Front snap-kick, double-punch 7,7A: Down-block, middle-block 8: Middle-punch 9,9A: Down-block, middle-block 10,10A: Double-punches stepping forward 11: Middle-block 12,12A: Two chasing-punches stepping forward 13: Middle-punch 14: Down-block 15,15A: Double-punch 16: Middle-block stepping back 17: Offering fist, Ready, Bow, Attention.

2A   3   3A   4   4A   4B

8   9   9A   10   10A

17

Fukyugata san-dan composed by Master Ueshiro in the 1960's is characterized by techniques emphasizing speed, combinations and strong, low stances.

The low stance indicates getting in and under your opponent, forcefully invading his space and disrupting his balance.

The blocks emphasize speed and combinations of defensive and offensive movements executed almost simultaneously.

This combination of techniques results in a most powerful flow of movement culminating in a devastating strike.

The kata maximizes one's strength and power and illustrates the "move forward" philosophy of the Shorin-ryu system.

33

Yakusoku kumite sandan.

Kumite and Weapons

1 What is the difference between yakusoku kumite and jiyu kumite?

2 Name the vulnerable striking points of the head and neck.

3 of the arms and hands.

4 of the front torso.

5 of the back torso.

6 of the front leg and foot.

7 of the back leg and foot.

8 Name the fist techniques.

9 the finger techniques.

10 the striking techniques.

11 the smashing techniques.

12 the blocking techniques.

13 the kicking techniques.

14 the intermediate movements.

15 Is the cat-stance better for defense or for attack?

16 What kind of attacks is the horse-stance good for?

17 Which are more powerful, kicks or punches?

35

18 What are the main parts of the foot that are used for striking?

19 In a kumite match, what is the Japanese word for one point scored and for one-half point scored?

20 Give the English for these Japanese words: tsuki, uchi, ate, geri.

21 How fast can a karate punch travel?

22 In first aid, what does the anagram RICE mean?

23 In executing a side kick (yoko-geri) will more force be generated if the upper body leans backwards or stays upright?

24 How much pressure will a focused karate punch deliver?

25 How much pressure does a kick deliver?

26 How strong are human bones?

27 According to Shorin-ryu philosophy, which is more important, kumite or kata?

28 What about in regards to self defense?

29 Is kumite or kata more realistic?

30 Is it necessary to practice kumite in order to be able to fight?

31 According to Shorin-ryu philosophy, which is more important jiyu or yakusoku kumite? Why?

32 Is protective equipment necessary to practice actual hitting?

33 Should we practice taking punches to get used to being hit?

34 If one never fights how will one learn to win?

35 Which is the most effective attack or strike?

"When the strike of a hawk breaks the body of its prey, it is because of timing. Strike the enemy as swiftly as a falcon strikes its target. It surely breaks the back of its prey for the reason that it awaits the right moment to strike; its moment is regulated. When torrential water tosses boulders, it is because of its momentum; thus the momentum of one skilled in war is overwhelming, and his attack precisely regulated. His potential is that of a fully drawn crossbow; his timing, the release of the trigger." SUN TZU

" The behavior and interactions of all people can be directly related to their ability to fight, to fight back, to preserve or improve their lives." PETER URBAN

" If your hand goes forth, withhold your temper; if your temper goes forth, withhold your hand." KARATE PRECEPT

36 the most effective defense?

37 What was the original use of the sai?

38 of the tuifa?

39 of the bo?

40 of the kama?

41 of the nunchaku?

42 What is the Japanese word for ancient weapon art?

43 Name five bo kata in use today.

44 How much time is required to develop skill with the bo or any weapon?

45 How much time is required to master the bo?

46 What is the bo's length?

47 Give the complete name of the bo.

48 How many weapons do the masters master?

49 To which Okinawan master are we indebted for our yakusoku kumite?

50 What does the phrase "Karate ni sente nashi" mean in English?

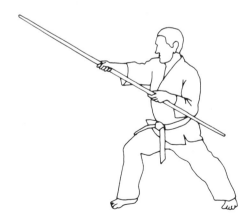

1 The first is pre-arranged and the second is free-style.

2-7 See diagram.

8 Jodan-zuki (upper punch), Chudan-zuki (middle punch), Gedan-zuki (lower punch), Kaka-zuki (square punch), Tomoe-zuki (circular block and punch), Sayu-zuki (double side punch), Kakushi-zuki (hidden fist punch), Oi-zuki (chasing punch), Wari-uke-zuki (split-block punch), Morote-zuki (augmented side punch), Gyaku-zuki (reverse punch).

9 Nukite-zuki (spear-hand thrust), Morote-nuki-zuki (Double spear-hand thrust), Shi-zuki (beak thrust).

10 Uraken-uchi (backfist strike), Kentsui-uchi (hammer fist strike), Shuto-uchi (knife hand strike), Kyobu shuto-uchi (chest knife-hand strike), Kyobu morote shuto-uchi (Chest double knife-hand strike), Kyobu-soete shuto-uchi (chest augmented knife-hand strike), Haito-uchi (reverse knife-hand strike).

11 Hiji-ate (elbow smash), Tate hiji-ate (upward elbow smash), Yoko hiji-ate (forward elbow smash), Sasae hiji-ate (supported elbow smash), Hiza-ate (knee smash), Shotei-ate (palm-heel smash), Jodan shotei-ate (upper palm-heel smash), Chudan shotei-ate (middle palm-heel smash), Gedan shotei-ate (lower palm-heel smash), Tomoe shotei-ate (circular palm-heel smash).

12 Jodan uke (upper block), Chudan soto-uke (middle outward block), Chudan yoko-uke (middle inner block), Gedan uke (lower block), Gedan yoko-barai-uke (lower sidward block), Sasae-uke (supported forearm block), Sayu-barai-uke (double lower side block), Jodan wari-uke (upper split block), Chudan wari-uke (middle split block), Jodan kosa-uke (upper cross block), Gedan kosa-uke (lower cross block), Morote soe-uke (augmented forearm

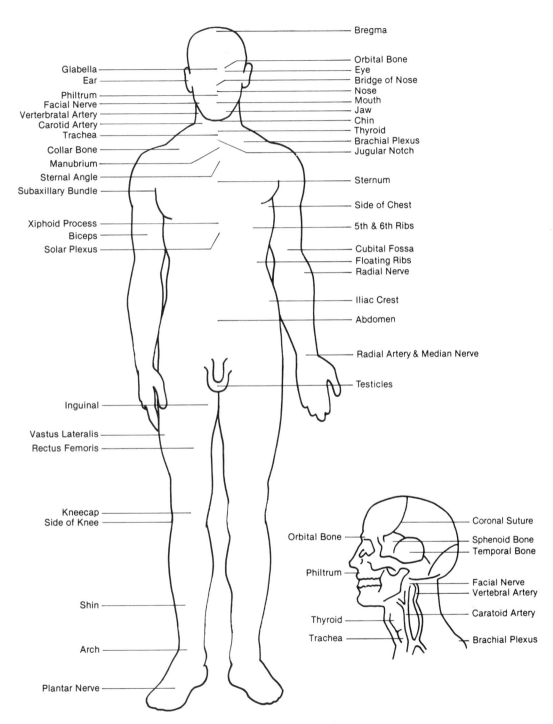

Bregma

Orbital Bone
Eye
Bridge of Nose
Nose
Mouth
Jaw
Chin
Thyroid
Brachial Plexus
Jugular Notch

Glabella
Ear
Philtrum
Facial Nerve
Verterbratal Artery
Carotid Artery
Trachea
Collar Bone
Manubrium
Sternal Angle
Subaxillary Bundle

Sternum

Side of Chest

Xiphoid Process
Biceps
Solar Plexus

5th & 6th Ribs

Cubital Fossa
Floating Ribs
Radial Nerve

Iliac Crest

Abdomen

Radial Artery & Median Nerve

Testicles

Inguinal

Vastus Lateralis
Rectus Femoris

Kneecap
Side of Knee

Coronal Suture
Sphenoid Bone
Temporal Bone

Orbital Bone

Philtrum

Facial Nerve
Vertebral Artery

Caratoid Artery

Shin

Thyroid
Trachea

Brachial Plexus

Arch

Plantar Nerve

PRESSURE POINTS, FRONT

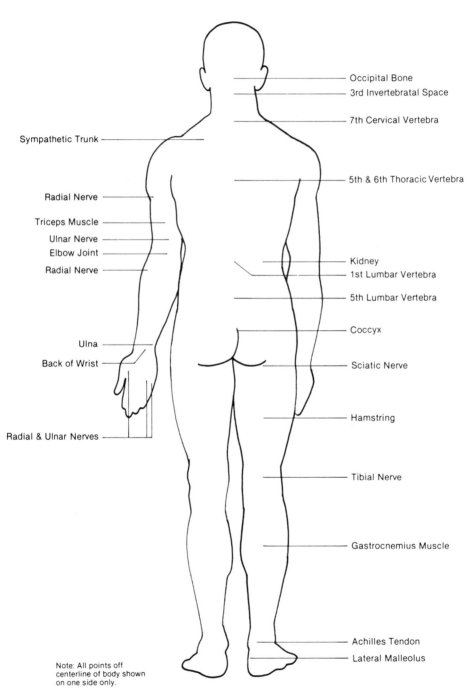

Occipital Bone
3rd Invertebratal Space
7th Cervical Vertebra

Sympathetic Trunk

5th & 6th Thoracic Vertebra

Radial Nerve
Triceps Muscle
Ulnar Nerve
Elbow Joint
Radial Nerve

Kidney
1st Lumbar Vertebra
5th Lumbar Vertebra

Coccyx

Ulna
Back of Wrist

Sciatic Nerve

Hamstring

Radial & Ulnar Nerves

Tibial Nerve

Gastrocnemius Muscle

Achilles Tendon
Lateral Malleolus

Note: All points off
centerline of body shown
on one side only.

PRESSURE POINTS, REAR

"The best swordsman in the world doesn't need to fear the second best swordsman in the world; no, the person for him to be afraid of is some ignorant antagonist who has never had a sword in his hand before; he doesn't do the thing he ought to do, and so the expert isn't prepared for him; he does the thing he ought not to do; and often it catches the expert out and ends him on the spot." MARK TWAIN

block), Chudan soto-mawashi-uke (middle sideward forearm block), Chudan soto-mawashi-uke (middle sidward round block), Morote-barai-uke (augmented lower block), Hazushi-uke (removing block), Otoshi-uke (dropping downward block), Chudan soto-shuto-uke (middle outward knife-hand block), Jodan uchi-shuto-uke (upper inner knife-hand block), Chudan yoko-shuto-uke (middle sideward knife-hand block), Gedan shuto-uke (lower knife-hand block), Gedan shuto yoko-barai-uke (lower sideward knife-hand slashing block), Chudan hasami-uke (middle scissors block), Makite-uke (winding knife-hand block), Magetori-barai-uke (rising upward both-hand knife block), Torite-uke (grasping hand block), Sagurite-uke (searching hand block), Gedan haito-yoko-uke (lower sideward reverse knife-hand block), Chudan shotei-uke (middle palm-heel block), Gedan shotei-uke (lower palm-heel block), Hiji-uke (elbow block), Hangetsu-barai-uke (half-moon foot block).

13 Kyobu-geri (chest kick), Fukubu-geri (abdomen kick), Kinteki-geri (groin kick), Sokuto-geri (foot-edge kick), Nidan-geri (flying front kick), Mae-geri (front snap kick).

14 Suiraken no kamae (drunkard fighting posture), Ryu-no-shita no kamae (dragon-tongue fighting posture), Sagurite no kamae (searching-hand fighting posture), Hotoke-gamae (Buddha-hand fighting posture), Tenshin no kamae (body-shifting fighting posture), Ura-gamae (cheating fighting posture).

15 Defense.

16 Attacks to the sides and front-lower body.

17 Each individual is different. Kicks generally are more powerful but not necessarily more effective. In kumite much depends on distance, attackers vulnerable area or target at the moment and

practitioners skill in a technique. It would be sadly misleading for everyone to think "my kick is more powerful than my punch." Fighting with this attitude would be a serious mistake.

18 Toes, instep, ball of foot, side, and heel.

19 Ippon is one point and waza-ari is one-half point.

20 Thrust (punch), strike, hit (smash), kick.

21 Forty-three feet per second generating power equal to 1,500 pounds.

22 REST, ICE, COMPRESSION, and ELEVATION.

23 Stays upright, the more one leans back the more power is dissipated.

24 700 foot pounds.

25 2100 foot pounds.

26 They are forty times stronger than concrete.

27 Kata is the essence of karate.

28 Kata.

29 Kata is the more real. You never hold back or control your technique. You never concern yourself with your attacker's strategy, just your attacker's technique of the moment.

30 No.

31 Yakusoku because it is more like kata in that you do not hold back or control your technique as much as in jiyu. Also you attack to a more correct "mai."

32 No, actual hitting can be done on makiwara and makiwara-type paraphernalia (trees, heavy bag, medicine bag, walls, tires, floors, etc.).

33 In karate one should never get accustomed to being hit or thrown down.

"The stillness in stillness is not the real stillness; only when there is stillness in movement does the universal rhythm manifest itself." TAOIST SAYING

"Control your emotion or it will control you." CHINESE ADAGE

"It is the mark of a rarely stable mind that antagonism cannot drive it to extremes."
C.H. COOLEY

"Power of mind is infinite while brawn is limited." KOICHI TOHEI

"For the uncontrolled there is no wisdom, nor for the uncontrolled is there the power of concentration; and for him without concentration there is no peace. And for the unpeaceful, how can there be happiness?" BHAGAVADGITA

34 By never fighting!

35 The one you practice most.

36 The one you need at the moment of an attack. It could be a strike, body-shifting, stepping back or forward, it could be verbal or psychological or it could even be a blocking (uke) technique.

37 To arrest criminals, hold back crowds and defend against sword attacks.

38 Millstone handle.

39 Carry loads.

40 Hand sickle.

41 Flail.

42 Kobujutsu.

43 There are many bo kata. As in all weapons they are individually developed by the high ranking sensei. Shorin-ryu is "karate" (empty hand system). The system does not dictate exact steps for weapons kata. Name five sensei who have composed bo kata and you have named five bo kata.

44 At least five years of practice several hours a day.

45 Ten years.

46 Six feet is the translation but it depends on the height of the individual.

47 Ro-ku sha-ku bo (six-foot staff).

48 One.

49 Choki Motobu.

50 "There is no first attack in karate."

Some Thoughts About Kumite

Kumite practice should be second to kata practice. It is almost impossible to simulate a real fighting situation. Improper practice, as in jyu-kumite, will dull the natural reflex and response to a threatening punch or kick. Using controlled techniques, as in tournament fighting, rather than blocking, jamming or body shifting, develops bad habits. Turning one's back to stop an opponent from scoring a point is another bad habit which is developed by improper training.

Correct distance for any given technique is very important in a fighting situation. In free style fighting it is almost impossible to use a full power technique at the proper range without doing serious damage to our opponent. Whenever a technique in free style results in a serious injury it is called an accident but in reality we train to do grievous bodily harm to our opponent.

Pre-arranged fighting is more conducive to the development of a proficient karateka. Our opponent in yakusoku kumite can more realistically block our full power technique. The use of metaphors, imagery and visualization of a real fight during this type of training further develops one's skills.

Arm and body conditioning kumite such as tanren kumite, naihanchi body testing, and maki-wara training, develop strong muscle tissue and conditions not only the outer body but the internal organs. Internal strengths are also developed from this practice of body conditioning.

So kumite is part of training but the kumite must be understood and care must be used as to the type of kumite. The student's body structure, physical conditioning, internal strenghts and weaknesses must be considered by the instructor and the competitors. Kata must be our primary means of training because kata considers naturally all of the above mentioned ingredients.

Some Thoughts About Weapons

Weapons, the farm implements in Okinawan karate are an extension of the karateka's body. Weapons training should only begin when the deshi attains black belt status.

Each karateka can develop only one weapon. This requires up to three hours practice daily and is reserved for the most serious and dedicated student of karate. It would take at least five years of this type of training and attitude before one first begins to properly feel or understand the use of the weapon.

Most practitioners learn or imitate the use of the weapon but never actually become skilled in its use. They subconsciously become discouraged and put the weapon aside until some future time.

Weapons techniques are developed through the practice of one weapon kata and one weapon. The kata are not as traditional as the empty hand kata but rather may be as numerous and different as the number of sensei or developers of the weapons kata. Each master of karate develops his weapon kata to fit his own physical and psychological makeup and his own interpretation of the most effective method of using the weapon.

Weapons training is not as exacting an art as are the more traditional empty hand kata. Rather, weapons kata are the result of conclusions of individual sensei and their own physical capabilities.

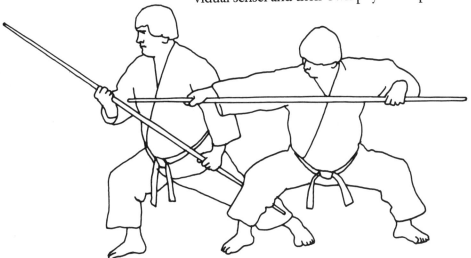

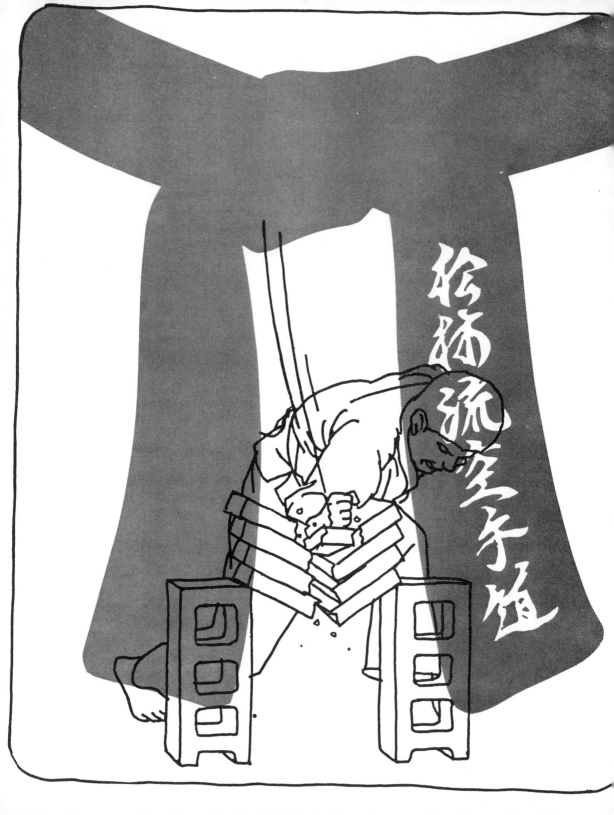

Karate

1 What do the various symbols on the Shorin-ryu patch signify?

2 What does the calligraphy under the Shorin-ryu patch say?

3 Can you recite the karate creed?

4 What is the most difficult task in teaching karate?

5 Approximately how many people are practicing karate in the United States?

6 What does the title "shihan" mean in English?

7 What are the four physical principles of Shorin-ryu karate?

8 What are the two psychological principals?

9 Who promotes the black belt ranks?

10 What are the qualifications for the title renshi?

11 for the title kyoshi?

12 for the title hanshi?

13 What does the Japanese word "bubishi" mean?

14 What is the Chinese term for martial arts?

15 How long must a student be able to hold a kiba-dachi posture without pain before being considered proficient?

16 What is the distinction between karate and karate-do?

17 Define kiai.

18 What does "hara" refer to?

19 What distinguishes Shorin-ryu karate from other karate styles?

20 How much of karate is mental and how much of it is physical?

21 What is the most important piece of equipment in the dojo?

"Buddha and the gods must lead us. But we must not rely on them completely."
MIYAMOTO MUSASHI

"When walking just walk, when sitting, just sit, above all, don't wobble."
YUN-MEN

"Freedom is primarily the acquisition of power; to be more exact, it is power which is not used." JEAN GRENIER

"As long as the soul stands erect it holds the body high and does not allow the years to touch it." NIKOS KAZANTZAKIS

"Because the eye gazes but can catch no glimpse of it, it is called elusive. Because the ear listens but cannot hear it, it is called rarefied. Because the hand feels for it but cannot find it, it is called the infinitesimal, its rising brings no light; its sinking no darkness. It is called Chi.
LAO TZU

"The best of all teachers are the ones who live the creed. To see good put into action is what everybody needs." ANONYMOUS

1 and 2 See diagram A, page 51.

3 "I come to you only with karate. My hands are empty, but I fear no man. Should I be forced to defend myself, my honor, or my principles; should it be a matter of right or wrong, life or death – then here are my weapons, my empty hands."

4 To instill a belief in the moral aspects of karate. To also discover what each individual's personal needs are and then develop each person to their highest physical, mental and spiritual potential.

5 1,500,000. (Louis Harris study, 1978)

6 Director, person in charge of a dojo.

7 1 Maximum muscular contraction. 2 Speed with which force is applied. 3 Conditioned reflex response. 4 Breath control.

8 1 A strong will to discourage brutality or violence from any source. 2 Willpower, confidence, endurance.

9 A black belt can be promoted by another black belt two grades higher, but ideally by the highest ranking sensei or master.

10 The title holder must be over thirty-five years old and have been a fifth dan at least two years.

11 The title holder must be at least forty-five years old and have been a renshi for ten years.

12 The title holder must be at least fifty-five years old and have been a kyoshi for fifteen years.

13 Martial arts spirit. From an ancient Chinese book on martial arts.

14 Wu-shu.

15 Two hours minimum. This may take several years to achieve.

16 Karate is a martial art using one's own body as a weapon and a means of self defense. Karate-do is a way of life in which one overcomes one's inner weakness by the practice of karate.

17 Kiai refers to a state of being where the mind, the spirit and the body are united and totally focused on the task at hand.

18 Hara refers to the stomach area, which in Japanese culture is considered to be the center of man's being. One's center.

19 Shorin-ryu karate is characterized by its natural movements which allow the practitioner to quickly adjust to any technique. Its body movements are more straightforward and natural than other karate styles. For example, practice of the front snap kick (mae-geri) will at the same time develop the side kick (yoko-geri) and the roundhouse kick (mawashi-geri). In Shorin-ryu there is no need to practice three different kicks because all three are essentially the same with minor adjustments of the kicking foot. Shorin-ryu is also unique in that ancient knowledge is preserved while at the same time modern physiological discoveries are constantly being added as they become known. An important principle of shorin-ryu which is distinctive is the idea, "when faced with an opponent, always move forward, never retreat." This idea applies equally as well to a life situation as to a fighting situation.

20 Karate is ninety percent mental and ten percent physical.

21 The mirror.

DIAGRAM A

JAPANESE
FOR
SHAO-LIN STYLE

GRAPHIC
REPRESENTATION
OF AN
EMPTY HAND

THE CROSSED SAI's
SYMBOLIZE
"WEAPONS"

KANJI
CHARACTERS
FOR
EMPTY HAND

GRAPHIC
REPRESENTATION
OF A
PINE TREE

THE "ROPE"
SYMBOLIZES
THE RYU-KYU
ISLANDS

CHINESE		JAPANESE	ENGLISH
CHUM		SHO	PINE
LUM		RIN	FOREST
LAO		RYU	STYLE

Some Thoughts About Karate
Physical Structure, Its Importance

"We are the sum total of our thoughts, everything we are we have thought first." BUDDHA

The most misunderstood aspect about karate technique is the concept of everyone being able to imitate stances and techniques. An important conclusion is that we should not look alike or be robot-like in our actions concerning karate.

A tall person would have a longer zenkutsu-dachi as compared to a shorter karateka. Someone with great muscular development, for example, may not be able to touch his fist to his forearm while demonstrating morote sae-uke properly. This would be because of a massive chest, pectorals and biceps. Consequently, a slim person's augmented forearm block would be and must be done quite differently. Someone with great strength in the development of the fingers should and is able to use nukite-waza effectively. To simply state the point, a person with a broken right hand should not use a migi-te-uchi.

The same holds true for one's current endurance level which changes with peaks and valleys throughout the years. Endurance is a consideration in the appearance of a kata and selection of a technique. Even the kata chosen can be changed, from one with twenty moves, to one with fifty-four moves accordingly.

The spirit or reason for doing a kata or going to battle will vary and will effect the outcome of our performance. Body structure, not photographs determine the how and why of any given movement and technique.

Here lies the importance of proper training and instruction! Recognizing that each one is as distinct as their signature. Learn the basics such as proper stance, balance, breathing, principles of technique, understanding of waza and then after developing the above mentioned principles, learn to develop your individual signature.

The natural flow of movement, again according to the dictates of one's body structure, strength, weakness, endurance and spirit, is the total essence of everything we seek from karate-do concerning kata and technique. This is why spirit is of utmost importance and why one should try to maintain an optimum level of spirit, endurance and strength in order to achieve maximum results from training. This principle applied to life itself allows us to accept any challenge if the need arises.

To reiterate: No, we are not and do not look like robots. Our kata, in the advanced stages, is as subtlely different as is our signatures. Our movements should flow naturally, then we can feel for ourselves what can easily be seen by the experienced eye, a correct or incorrect technique.

Humble Mind

"Every creative act involves...a new innocence of perception, liberated from the cataract of accepted belief."   ARTHUR KOESTLER

There is much more to a dojo than training and the development of technique and strength. The realization that the most powerful human being in the world can be struck down in a fraction of a second graphically shows that power goes beyond physical strength.

The teaching of humility is of much greater importance than the teaching of physical techniques. This is why we bow and show respect for others in the dojo. Bowing is a ritual courtesy displayed during karate practice, but it is also an important aspect of our training which must extend beyond the practice and beyond the dojo. We become stronger and more powerful in the true sense of the word through our deeds and through respect for ourselves and for others.

Throughout the ages the most powerful men on earth had little if any physical strength. They had powerful minds and thoughts. They were part of a powerful group. When we take the time to help others, we grow stronger ourselves. As our group grows stronger, every person affiliated with that group grows stronger. If the group is weak then so are the individuals in it.

The secret is to make your group stronger and

so you as an individual grow stronger. No one achieves anything alone.

This is karate-do philosophy as well as the philosophy of the great minds of the past.

Spiritual Energy

"The most powerful force on earth is the use of metaphors in the form of imagery." ARISTOTLE

The application of the thoughts of the mind is the secret of great feats. Philosophers from different geographical locations and different time periods recognized this as a truth.

In karate the mind is recognized as the catalyst to perfection. Through visualization, we first picture ourselves doing exceptional kata before it can be physically performed. Because of this practice we then can progress satisfactorily.

Through imagery we gain spirit and strength in ourselves. Kata itself is imagery and a metaphor in its simplest state and is also most perfect according to our minds, and in direct relation to the fortitude of our thoughts.

The Okinawan masters also propagated their art throughout the centuries emphasizing the importance of training and the development of one's mind, thoughts and spirit. These *must* be combined and transformed into acts and deeds in our humble contacts with others.

CHINESE		JAPANESE	ENGLISH
CHUM		SHO (MATSU)	PINE
LUM		RIN (BAYASHI)	FOREST
LAO		RYU	STYLE
HUN		KARA	EMPTY
SHO		TE	HAND
DO		DO	WAY

Black Belt Inscription

奉我的空手道來保護人生存亡

免我了懼怕也不需任何

從來者面對正義樂生

Japanese Terminology

Achi	Arch of foot
Age	Rising
Ananku	The twelfth kata in Shorin-ryu karate
Anza	Cross-leg sitting
Arigato	Thank-you
Ashi	Foot
Atama	Head
Atemi-waza	Breaking technique
Ate-waza	Smashing technique
Barai	Sweep
Bo	Staff
Bojutsu	Bo technique
Bubishi	Martial art spirit
Budo	Japanese martial arts
Bun-kai	Application of kata
Bushi	Japanese warrior
Bushido	"The way of the warrior"
Chinto	The eighteenth kata of Shorin-ryu karate
Chishi	An ancient form of dumbell, one-sided weight
Chokuritsu-fudo-dachi	Formal attention stance
Chudan	Middle
Chudan hasami-uke	Middle scissors block
Chudan shotei-uke	Middle palm heel block
Chudan soto-mawashi-uke	Middle sideward round block

Chishi

57

Chudan soto-shuto-uke	Middle outward knife-hand block
Chudan soto-uke	Middle outward block
Chudan uchi-uke	Middle inner block
Chudan wari-uke	Middle split block
Chudan yoko-shuto-uke	Middle sideward knife-hand block
Chudan yoko-uke	Middle sideward block
Chudan-uke	Middle block
Chudan-zuki	Middle punch
Chusoku	Ball of foot
Dan	Grade (black belt)
Dachi	Stance
Denzook	No count
Deshi	Karate student (below black belt level)
Do	Way–spiritual path. Means both way and object. The object is also the way.
Dojo	Sacred hall of learning
Dozo	Please
Doryo	Magnamanity. (One of the six virtues of the warrior)
Fudo	Posture and attitude, immutability (one of the six virtues of the warrior).
Fukubu-geri	Abdomen kick
Fukyugata	Basic
Fukyugata ichi	The first kata in Shorin-ryu karate.
Fukyugata ni	The second kata in Shorin-ryu karate.
Fukyugata san	The third kata in Shorin-ryu karate.
Furitsuki	Round house punch
Gedan	Lower
Gedan haito-yoko-uke	Lower sideward reverse knife-hand block
Gedan kosa-uke	Lower cross block
Gedan shotei-uke	Lower palm heel block
Gedan shuto-uke	Lower knife hand block

Chudan soto-shuto-uke

Chudan wari-uke

Chudan yoko-shuto-uke

Gedan haito-yoko-uke

Gedan shotei-uke

Gedan kosa-uke

Gedan shuto-uke

58

Gedan shuto yoko-barai-uke

Gedan yoko-barai-uke

Hangetsu-barai-uke

Hasami-uke

Gedan shuto yoko-barai-uke	Lower sideward knife-hand slashing block
Gedan-uke	Lower block
Geden yoko-barai-uke	Lower sideward block
Gedan-zuki	Lower punch
Genshin	Intuitive ability to anticipate an attack
Geri	Kick
Gerikata	Kicking techniques
Gi	Karate uniform
Giri	The duty (one of the six virtues of the warrior)
Go	Five
Go-dan	Fifth degree black belt
Goju-ryu	"Hard-soft" style, one of the major karate styles from Naha, Okinawa
Gojushiho	The seventeenth kata of Shorin-ryu karate
Go-kyu	Two green tips on white belt
Gyaku	Reverse
Hachi	Eight
Hachi-dan	Eigth degree black belt
Hachiji-dachi	Open leg stance
Hachimaka	Headband
Haisoku	Instep
Haito-uchi	Reverse knife-hand strike
Haito-uke	Reverse knife-hand block
Hajime	Begin
Hangetsu-barai-uke	Half-moon foot block
Hanshi	Title given after fifteen years as kyoshi. Must be at least fifty-five years old.
Hara	In Japanese culture, the center of a man's being or consciousness. Located approximately two inches below the navel.
Hasami-uke	Scissors block
Hazushi-uke	Removing block
Heisoku-dachi	Closed-foot stance

Hidari	Left
Hiji-ate	Elbow smash
Hiji-uke	Elbow block
Hiza-ate	Knee smash
Hotoke-gamae	Buddha-hand fighting posture
Iaigoshi-dachi	Kneeling stance
Ichi	One
Ichiban	Number one
Ik-kyu	Black tips on brown belt
Ippon	One point
Ippon-ashi-dachi	One-leg stance
Jigotai-dachi	Wide-open leg stance
Jyu	Free style
Jo	Short stick
Jodan	Upper
Jodan kosa-uke	Upper cross block
Jodan uchi-shuto-uke	Upper inner knife-hand block
Jodan uke	Upper block
Jodan wari-uke	Upper split block
Josokutei	Ball of foot
Jodan-zuki	Upper punch
Ju	Flexibility
Ju	Ten
Ju-dan	Tenth-degree black belt
Jun shizentai-dachi	Quasi-natural stance
Jutsu	Science, technique
Kakato	Heel
Kaku	Square
Kaku-zuki	Square punch
Kakushi-zuki	Hidden fist punch
Kama	Hand sickle
Kamaekata	Ready stances
Kami	Heavy earthenware jars
Kanji	Chinese and Japanese ideograms

Hotoke-gamae

Jodan-zuki

Kaku-zuki

Kakushi-zuki

Kara	Empty
Kara-zuki	Empty-hand punching
Karate	Empty-handed self-defense art
Karate-do	Way of karate
Karateka	Proficient practitioner of karate
Kata	Form – an organized series of pre-arranged defensive and offensive movements symbolizing an imaginary fight between several opponents and performed in a geometrical pattern. Handed down and perfected by masters of a system of karate.

Kentsui-uchi

Kasane-uchi	Double knife-hand
Keikoken	Forefinger knuckle
Kentsui	Hammerfist
Kentsui-uchi	Hammer-fist strike
Ki	Vital energy
Kiai	Spirit continuing force or spirit. Killing technique. Has nothing to do with shout or noise or sound.
Kiba-dachi	Horse-stance
Kime	Focus
Kinteki-geri	Groin kick
Kio-tsuke	Attention
Kobayashi-ryu	"Young forest" style, Shorin-ryu
Kobujutsu	Ancient weapon art
Koken	Wrist
Kokutsu-dachi	Back-leg-bent stance
Kosa	Cross
Kosa-dachi	Cross-leg stance
Kosa-uke	Cross block
Koshi-o-ireru	"Putting in the hip"
Ku	Nine
Ku-dan	Ninth degree black belt
Kumite	Fight
Kusanku	The nineteenth kata of Shorin-ryu karate and most difficult.
Kyobu	Chest
Kyobu-geri	Chest kick

Kosa-dachi

Kyobu shuto-uchi	Chest knife hand strike
Kyoshi	Title given only after ten years as a renshi. Must be at least 45 years old.
Kyu	Rank
Kyusho	Vital point
Ma-ai	Distancing, the ability to intuitively establish the correct distance between oneself and one's opponent – concentration.
Mae	Front
Mae-geri	Front kick
Magetori-barai-uke	Rising upward both-hand knife-block
Makite-uke	Winding knife-hand block
Makiwara	Striking board
Matsubayashi-ryu	"Pine forest" style, Shorin-ryu.
Matsumura-orthodox	One of the major Okinawan karate styles
Mawashi	Round
Mawashi-geri	Round-house kick
Mawate	Turn
Migi	Right
Morote-barai-uke	Augmented lower block
Morote-nuki-zuki	Double spear-hand thrust
Morote-soe-uke	Augmented forearm block
Morote-zuki	Augmented side punch
Mushin	No-mind
Naha-te	Karate from Naha, Okinawa
Nakatakaken	Mid-finger extended knuckle fist
Naname zenkutsu-dachi	Slanted front-leg-bent stance
Neko-ashi-dachi	Cat stance
Naihanchi-dachi	Straddle-leg stance
Naihanchi nidan	The tenth kata in Shorin-ryu karate.
Naihanchi sandan	The eleventh kata in Shorin-ryu karate.
Naihanchi shodan	The ninth kata in Shorin-ryu karate.
Ni	Two

Kyobu shuto-uchi

Mae-geri

Morote-zuki

62

Ni-dan	Second degree black belt
Nidan-geri	Flying front kick
Ni-kyu	Brown belt
Ninyo	Magnamanity, on higher level than doryo (one of the six virtues of the warrior)
Nukite-zuki	Spear-hand thrust
Nunchaku	Flail
Obi	Belt or sash
Oi-zuki	Chasing, lunge punch
Onegai-shimasu	Please teach us
Onsha	Generosity, tolerance (one of the six virtues of the warrior)
Otoshi -uke	Dropping downward block
Oyo-tan-ren	All basic techniques
Passai	The sixteenth kata in Shorin-ryu karate
Pinan	Intermediate
Pinan godan	The eighth kata in Shorin-ryu karate
Pinan nidan	The fifth kata in Shorin-ryu karate
Pinan sandan	The sixth kata in Shorin-ryu karate
Pinan shodan	The fourth kata in Shorin-ryu karate
Pinan yondan	The seventh kata in Shorin-ryu karate
Rei	Bow
Renshi	Title given after two years as godan. Must be at least 35 years old. Title/Spelling/Pronunciation of Renshi is Denshi in the Shorin-ryu karate USA organization
Rohai	The fourteenth kata in Shorin-ryu karate
Roku	Six
Roku-dan	Sixth degree black belt
Rokushakubo	Six-foot staff
Ro-kyu	One green tip on white belt
Ryu	Martial tradition
Ryu-no-shita no kamae	Dragon-tongue fighting posture
Sagurite no kamae	Searching-hand fighting posture

Nukite-zuki

Oi-zuki

Ryu-no-shita no kamae

Sagurite no kamae

Sagurite-uke	Searching-hand block
Sai	Ancient weapon used to defend against sword attacks
Samurai	Japanese warrior
San	Three
San-dan	Third degree black belt
San-kyu	Brown tips on green belt
Sasae hiji-ate	Supported elbow smash
Sasae-uke	Supported forearm block
Sashi	Iron hand grip
Sayu-barai-uke	Double lower side block
Sayu-zuki	Double side punch
Seiken	Fist
Seiken-ude-uke	Forearm block
Seiken-waza	Fist technique
Seiza	Sit, kneeling
Semekata	Attacking techniques
Sempai	Senior
Sensei	Teacher or master
Sensei-ni-rei	All bow to sensei
Shiai	Contest
Shi	Three
Shi-dan	Third degree black belt
Shichi	Seven
Shichi-dan	Seventh degree black belt
Shihan	Director
Shiki	Resolution (one of the six virtues of the warrior)
Shinden-ni-rei	All bow to those who came before us
Shinpan	Judge, referee
Shinsa	Examination
Shizentai-dachi	Natural stance
Shi-zuki	Beak thrust
Shobayashi-ryu	"Small forest" style, Shorin-ryu
Sho-dan	First degree black belt
Shorei-ryu	Naha-te karate
Shorin-ryu	"Shao-lin" style, Shuri-te karate

Sai

Sayu-zuki

Seiza

Shi-zuki

Samurai warrior.

Sensei-ni-mawate	Turn to sensei
Shotei-ate	Palm-heel smash
Shotei-uke	Palm-heel block
Shotu-mate	Stop, shut-up
Shuri-te	Karate from Shuri, Okinawa
Shuto	Open (knife hand)
Shuto-uchi	Knife-hand strike
Shuto-uke	Knife-hand block
Sokko	Instep
Sokuto-geri	Foot edge kick
Soto	Outward
Soto-hachiji	Open leg
Suirakan no kamae	Drunkard fighting posture
Suki	Opening
Tameshiwari	Breaking technique
Tanren kumite	Arm Training
Tanden	Source of vital energy
Tate hiji-ate	Upward elbow smash
Te	Hand
Tenshin	Body shifting
Tenshin no kamae	Body shifting fighting posture
Tetsugeta	Iron clogs
Tobi yoko-geri	Flying side kick
Tode	Ancient Okinawan fighting art
Tomari-te	Karate from Tomari, Okinawa
Tomoe	Circular
Tomoe shotei-ate	Circular palm-heel smash
Tomoe-zuki	Circular block and punch
Torite-uke	Grasping hand block
Toshokai	Meeting to encourage discussion
Tsuki	Punch
Tsuki-uke	Punching block
Tsuki-waza	Punching technique
Tsumasaki	Tips of toes

Suiraken no kamae

Tate hiji-ate

Tomoe shotei-ate

Tomoe-zuki

Tuifa

Uraken

Wari-uke-zuki

Yoko hiji-ate

Tuifa	Millstone handle
Uchi-waza	Striking techniques
Ude	Forearm
Ude-uke	Forearm block
Uechi-ryu	One of the major karate styles from Naha, Okinawa
Uke	Block
Ukekata	Blocking techniques
Ura-gamae	Cheating fighting posture
Uraken	Backfist
Uraken-uchi	Backfist strike
Ushiro	Back
Ushiro-geri	Back kick
Ushiro hiji-ate	Backward elbow smash
Wankan	The thirteenth kata in Shorin-ryu karate
Wanshu	The fifteenth kata in Shorin-ryu karate
Wari-uke-zuki	Split-block punch
Waza	Technique, skill
Waza-ari	One-half point
Yakusoku	Pre-arranged
Yama-zuki	U-punch
Yame	Stop
Yoi	Ready
Yoko	Side
Yoko-geri	Sidekick
Yoko hiji-ate	Forward elbow smash
Yoko-tobi-geri	Flying side kick
Yon-dan	Fourth degree black belt
Yon-kyu	Green belt
Yubi-waza	Finger techniques
Zanshin	Ready mind
Zazen	Sitting meditation
Zenkutsu-dachi	Front-leg-bent stance
Zenkutsu-dachi gedan-barai-uke	Front-leg-bent stance lower block
Zuki	Punching

Appendix

Warm-Ups

Half Squats   Stand up straight, hands on hips and bend knees to half squats. Feet are shoulder width apart.

Full Squats   Stand up straight, hands on hips, feet separated, up on toes. Squat all the way to the floor. (Also, be able to squat with feet flat on floor.)

Leg Raises   Stand up straight, hands outstretched each 45°, shoulder height. Lift legs up with knees straight bringing them up on a line just inside the hands. Move hands to straight in front of the shoulders and lift legs up between the hands. Then turn 45° to the left, bring hands straight out to the sides and lift legs up again bring them up on a line just inside the hands.

Neck Exercise   First twist left and right, then chin to chest and then to ceiling, then ear to shoulder, then circle.

Side Stretching   Separate legs. Fold one hand into fist position and raise it to under arm. Take the other arm, make a fist and stretch arm overhead, bending to the opposite side. Repeat other side.

Leg Stretch 1   Separate legs past shoulder width, stretch hands and arms straight up overhead, bend forward touching the floor with the hands. Stretch back with fists supporting the lower back, repeat.

Toe Touch   Separate feet, extend arms straight out to the sides, parallel to the deck. Twist to the left, reach right hand and arm straight up overhead, bend over, touch the left toe, come up to starting position, arms extended out to the sides. Repeat to the opposite side.

Leg Stretch 2   Separate legs past shoulders width. Cross/fold arms in front of chest, bend forward bringing elbows and head towards the floor and back up on each count.

Jump Up/Side Straddle Hops   Feet together. Hands loose at side. Jump and separate feet. Jump and bring feet together. Repeat.

Cross-over Hops   Feet apart. Cross left foot in front. Repeat. Then repeat with right foot crossing in front. Then repeat, alternating feet.

Forward Jumps   Left foot forward, right foot back. Reverse feet. Repeat.

This series is done to loosen up before each class. The series is always the same. Each student is expected to try to do each exercise to the best of his ability. No one is expected to do them all 100% correctly the first time. Each series starts with the left side, and continues with repetitions of 10.

Okinawan Karate Evolution

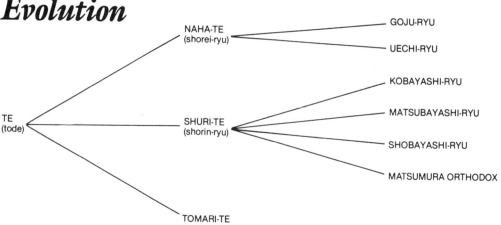

Major Shorin-ryu Branches

Ankichi Arakaki Chotoku Kyan Choki Motobu Taro Shimabuku	Shoshin Nagamine (founder)	**MATSUBAYASHI-RYU** (pine forest style)
Choki Motobu Chojun Miyagi	Chotoku Kyan (founder)	**SHOBAYASHI-RYU** (small forest style)
Yasutsune Itosu	Chosin Chibana (founder)	**KOBAYASHI-RYU** (young forest style)
Bushi Matsumura	Hohan Soken (founder)	**MATSUMURA ORTHODOX**

Stances

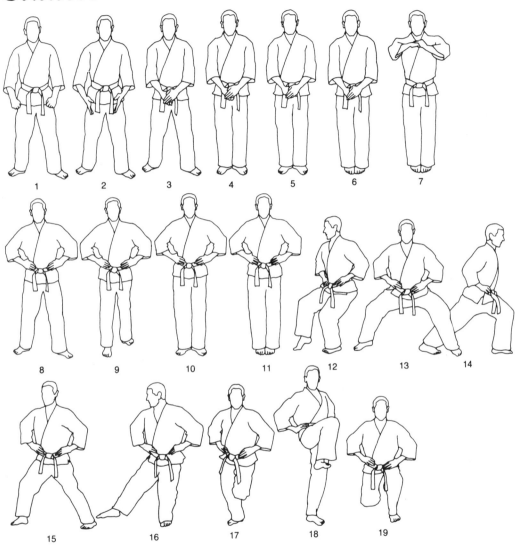

Kamaekata (Ready Stances 1 through 7) 1,2,3 Soto-hachiji shizentai-dachi (Open-leg natural stance) 1: Pinan and Gojushiho 2: Rohai 3: Kusanku **4,5** Chokuritsu-fudo-dachi (Formal attention stance) 4: Fukyugata 5: Wankan **6,7 Heisoku-dachi (Closed-foot stance)** 6: Naihanchi, Passai, Chinto and Ananku 7: Wanshu **Dachikata (Stances 8 through 19** 8,9 Shizentai-dachi (Natural Stance) 8: Soto-Hachiji Shizentai-dachi (Open-leg natural stance) 9: Migi-ashi-mae Shizentai-dachi (Right-foot-front natural stance) Hidari-ashi-mae if left foot is forward **10, 11, 12 Jun shizentai-dachi (Quasi-natural stance)** 10: Chokuritsu-fudo-dachi (Formal attention stance) 11: Heisoku-dachi (Closed-foot stance) 12: Neko-ashi-dachi (Cat stance) **13 Jigotai-dachi (Wide open-leg stance)** Naihanchi-dachi (Straddle-leg stance) same as 13 but with feet parallel instead of forty-five degrees **14** Zenkutsu-dachi (Front-leg-bent stance) **15 Naname zenkutsu-dachi (Slanted front-leg-bent stance) 16** Kokutsu-dachi (Back-leg-bent stance) **17** Kosa-dachi (Cross-leg stance) **18** Ippon-ashi-dachi (One-leg stance) **19** Iaigoshi-dachi (Kneeling stance)

71

Attacking Techniques

Semekata (Attacking techniques) 1 through 11 Seiken waza (Fist technique) 1: Jodan-zuki (Upper punch) 2: Chudan-zuki (Middle punch) 3: Gedan-zuki (Lower punch) 4 and 5: Kaku-zuki (Square punch) 6: Tomoe-zuki (Circular block and punch) 7: Kakushi-zuki (Hidden fist punch) 8: Sayu-zuki (Double side punch) 9: Oi-zuki (Chasing punch) 10: Wari-uke-zuki (Split-block punch) 11: Morote-zuki (Augmented-side punch) **12,13,14, Yubi waza (Finger technique)** 12: Nukite-zuki (Spear-hand thrust) 13: Morote-nuki-zuki (Double spear-hand thrust) 14: Shi-zuki (Beak thrust)

15 through 20 Uchi waza (Striking techniques) 15: Uraken-uchi (Backfist strike) 16: Kentsui-uchi (Hammer-fist strike) 17: Kyobu shuto-uchi (Chest knife-hand strike) 18: Kyobu morote shuto-uchi (Chest double knife-hand strike) 19: Kyubu-soete shuto-uchi (Chest augmented knife-hand strike) 20: Haito-uchi (Reverse knife-hand strike) **21 through 29 Ate-waza (Smashing technique)** 21: Tate-hiji-ate (Upward elbow smash) 22: Yoko hiji-ate (Forward elbow smash) 23: Ushiro hiji-ate (Backward elbow smash) 24: Sasae hiji-ate (Supported elbow smash) 25: Hiza-ate (Knee smash) 26: Jodan shotei-ate (Upper palm-heel smash) 27: Chudan shotei-ate (Middle palm-heel smash) 28: Tomoe shotei-ate (Circular palm-heel smash) 29: Gedan shotei-ate (Lower palm-heel smash)

Blocking Techniques

Ukekata (Blocking techniques) 1 through 17 1: Jodan-uke (upper block) 2: Chudan soto-uke (Middle block) 3: Chudan yoko-uke (Middle sideward block) 4: Chudan uchi-uke (Middle inner block) 5: Sayu-barai-uke (Double lower side block) 6: Gedan-uke (Lower block) 7: Sasae-uke (Supported block) 8: Gedan yoko-barai-uke (Lower sideward block) 9: Jodan wari-uke (Upper split block) 10: Chudan wari-uke (Middle split block) 11: Jodan kosa-uke (Upper cross block) 12: Gedan kosa-uke (Lower cross block) 13: Morote soe-uke (Augmented forearm block) 14: Chudan soto-mawashi-uke (Middle sideward round block) 15: Morote-barai-uke (Augmented lower block) 16: Hazushi-uke (Removing block) 17: Otoshi-uke (Dropping downward block) **18 and 19 Shotei-uke (Palm-heel block)** 18: Chudan shotei-uke (Middle palm-heel block) 19: Gedan shotei-uke (Lower palm-heel block)

20 through 30 Shuto and haito-uke (Knife-hand and reverse knife-hand blocks) 20: Chudan soto-shuto-uke (Middle outward knife-hand block) 21: Jodan uchi-shuto-uke (Upper inner knife-hand block) 22: Chudan yoko-shuto-uke (Middle sideward knife-hand block) 23: Gedan shuto-uke (Lower knife-hand block) 24: Gedan shuto yoko-barai-uke (Lower sideward knife-hand slashing block) 25: Chudan hasami-uke (Middle scissors block) 26: Makite-uke (Winding knife-hand block) 27: Torite-uke (Grasping-hand block) 28: Magetori-barai-uke (Rising upward both-hand knife block) 29: Sagurite-uke (Searching-hand block) 30: Gedan haito-yoko-uke (Lower sideward reverse knife-hand block) **31: Hiji-uke (Elbow block) 32: Hangetsu-barai-uke (Half-moon foot block)**

Kicking Techniques

Gerikata (Kicking Techniques) 1: Fukubu-geri (Abdomen kick) 2: Kyobu-geri (Chest kick) 3: Sokuto-geri (Foot-edge kick) 4: Kinteki-geri (Groin kick) 5 and 5A: Nidan-geri (Flying front kick)

Intermediate Movements

Intermediate movements 1: Suiraken no kamae (Drunkard fighting posture) 2: Ryu-no-shita no kamae (Dragon-tongue fighting posture) 3: Hotoke-gamae (Buddha-hand fighting posture) 4: Tenshin no kamae (Body-shifting fighting posture) 5: Ura-gamae (Cheating fighting-posture) 6: Sagurite no kamae (Searching-hand fighting posture)

Weight Distribution

Shizentai-dachi   The weight is on the balls of the feet. Fifty percent on the forward foot and fifty percent on the rear foot. The body projects slightly forward with the knees slightly bent.

Jigotai-dachi   The feet are forty-five degrees with the weight equally distributed. The weight is towards the heels. The upper body is relaxed and square in front.

Zenkutsu-dachi   The front leg is bent and the knee is over the toes. The rear leg knee is locked out. Seventy percent of the weight is on the front leg, thirty percent is on the rear leg.

Neko-ashi-dachi   From shizentai-dachi drop straight down. Put ninety percent of the weight on the rear foot and ten percent on the front foot. Put most of the weight on the rear of the rear foot.

Shorin-ryu Belt System

	white belt	green tips one-ro-kyu two-go-kyu	green belt yon-kyu	brown tips san-kyu
minimum time in dojo		two months	twelve months	eighteen months
average time at level	two to six months	six months to one year as a green tip	six months to one and a half years as a green belt	six months to two years as a brown tip
meaning of level	beginning student learns customary respect and behavior	starting to build a good foundation of self discipline endurance and health	this level is the backbone of the dojo... student shows much spirit and has displayed a sincere desire and effort to learn	becomes more aware and appreciative of traditional karate techniques. sees they are starting to work
general summary of test requirements	no testing, but student must display a willingness to learn	first and second kata *plus* an understanding of basic moves	third kata *plus* basic fighting skills *plus* simple breaking technique	first and second pinan katas *plus* knowledge of more sophisticated move and stances

own belt kyu	black tips ik-kyu	black belt sho-dan	as a black belt one continues to learn and perfect karate skills old and new...the karate person's skills will live with him/her forever... a black belt's knowledge is priceless... weapons, many more interesting and exciting katas and fighting skills will be learned as the student advances in the black belt degrees
enty-four onths	thirty-six months	discretion of Hanshi Robert Scaglione	
e year to ee years as brown belt	discretion of Hanshi as a black tip	three to six years as a sho-dan	
splays strength amina, balance d coordination his performance... ginning to learn d apply teaching ills	displays much confidence in handling himself and others...learns patience and perserverance... shows the most spirit	becomes an accomplished karate student appreciative of all aspects of karate... eager to share his/her knowledge with others	
ird, fourth and th pinan katas us fighting skills us breaking chnique	first naihanchi kata	second and third naihanchi katas, ananku *plus* special kata wankan *plus* fighting skills and breaking technique	

Martial Arts Systems

COUNTRY	SYSTEM	FOUNDER	DATE
Brazil	Capoeira		
Burma	Bando		
China	Choy Li Fut	Chan Hueng	1836
	Hung Gar	Hung Hei Goon	
	Hsing I Chuan	Yueh-Fei	11th Century
	Pa Kua Chang	Tung Hai Chuna	
	Sil Lum		
	Tai Chi Chuan	Chang San-Feng	13th Century
	Wing Chung	Ng Mui	18th Century
France	Savate		17th Century
Greece	Pankration		
Hawaii	Lua		
	Kosho-Ryu-Kempo		
India	Bandesh		
	Kalarippayatt		12th Century
	Vajramushti		
	Varrmannie		
Indonesia	Pentjak		
	Silak		
Japan	Akido	Morihei Ueshiba	1927
	Iaido		
	Judo	Jigaro Kano	1882
	Ju Jutsu	Takenouchi Hisamori	1532
	Kendo		17th Century
	Kyokushinkai	Masutatsu Oyama	20th Century
	Kyu-do		
	Naginata-do		
	Ninjutsu		
	Shotokan	Gichin Funakoshi	1922
	Shorinji Kempo		
	Sumo		
	Wado-Ryu	Otsuka	
Java	Ahntook Ken		
Korea	Hapkido	Yong Sui Choi	1950
	Hwarang Do	Won Kwang Bobsa	2nd Century
	Tang Soo Do	Hwang Kee	20th Century
	Tae Kwon Do	Hwang Kee	1945
Malaya	Bersilat		

COUNTRY	SYSTEM	FOUNDER	DATE
Philippines	Kau		8th Century
	Arnis		
Russia	Sambo		
Ryukyu	Goju-Ryu	Chojun Miyagi	1917
	Isshin-Ryu	Tatsuo Shimabuku	1955
	Koei-Kan	Elzo Onishi	1952
	Naha-Te		
	Shito-Ryu	Mabuni Kenwa	1926
	Shorenji Kempo		
	Shorin-Ryu	Bushi Matsumura	1820
	Kobayashi	Choshin Chibana	1930
	Matsubayashi	Shoshin Nagamine	1940
	Matsumura Orthodox	Hohan Soken	1920
	Shobayashi	Chotoku Kyan	1910
	Shuri Te	Bushi Matsumura	1820
	Tode		
	Tomari Te		
	Uechi-Ryu	Kanbun Uechi	1920
Thailand	Muay Thai		

Savate

Sumo

81

How To Tie A Belt

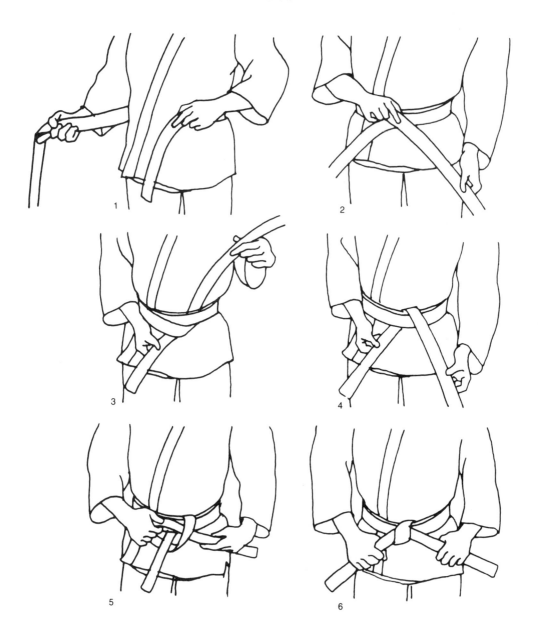

How To Fold A Gi

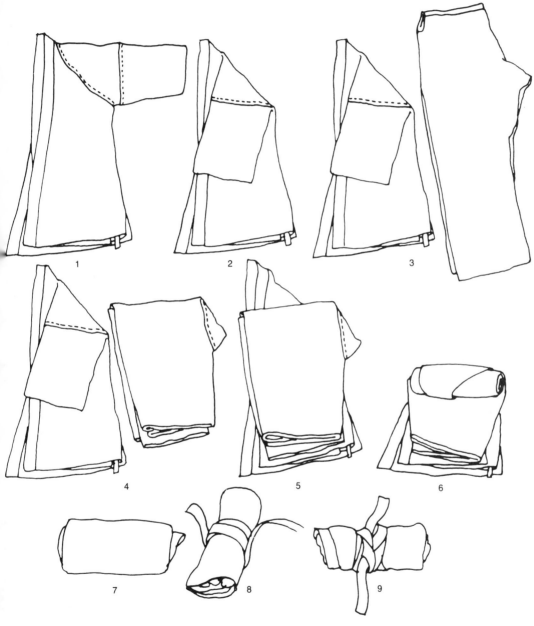

Dojo Rules

1 Always show courtesy to all.
2 Address your instructor as sensei.
3 Bow to the sensei when entering or leaving the school.
4 When a black belt instructor enters or leaves the deck in uniform for the first time, the senior student stops the activity on the deck and orders the students to attention.
5 No smoking in the school.
   No wearing of jewelry or other ornaments on the deck during a class.
   No food or drink allowed on the deck.
   No talking or laughing while class is in session.
   No profanity.
6 Keep your uniform clean.
7 Keep your fingernails and toenails short.
8 Refrain from misusing your knowledge.
9 Do not consume alcoholic beverages before class, your timing could be affected and cause injury.
10 Do not leave the deck during a class without your sensei's permission.
11 Students bow to each other before and after each practice.
12 Strive to promote the true spirit of the martial arts by:
   Character, mental development
   Health, physical development
   Skill, proficiency in karate
   Respect, courtesy to others
   Humility, be aware of your shortcomings.
13 Each student is responsible for keeping his own attendance sheet.
14 Always show courtesy to all.

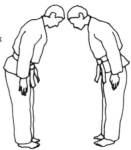 

Japanese Counting

	JAPANESE	PRONUNCIATION
1	ICHI	ITCH
2	NI	KNEE
3	SAN	SAN
4	SHI	SHE
5	GO	GO
6	ROKU	ROW
7	SHICHI	SHE
8	HACHI	HATCH
9	KU	CUE
10	JU	JEW

Vital Statistics

STARTED TRAINING

DATE _____ AGE _____ WEIGHT _____

FIRST DOJO

NAME _____

CITY _____ STATE _____

SECOND

NAME _____

CITY _____ STATE _____

OTHERS _____

_____

_____

FIRST SENSEI _____

SECOND _____

THIRD _____

OTHERS _____

_____

_____

PROMOTED TO

RO-KYU _____ GO-KYU _____ YON-KYU _____ SAN-KYU _____

NI-KYU _____ IK-KYU _____ SHO-DAN _____ NI-DAN _____

SAN-DAN _____ YON-DAN _____ GO-DAN _____ ROKU-DAN _____

SHICHI-DAN _____ HACHI-DAN _____ KU-DAN _____ JU-DAN _____

TOURNAMENT

NAME _____ PLACE _____ DATE _____ TROPHY _____

_____ _____ _____ _____

_____ _____ _____ _____

Black Belts Promoted by Master Ansei Ueshiro 1962-1991

GEORGE ALDRICH
JORGE ANDION
RICK ANNICHIARICO
SCOTT ASHLEY
JOE AVELLA
DAVID BAKER
BUZZY BAUMAN
MARK BELLUSCI
DAN BENGEL
STEVEN BEVIL
ANN BILLOCK
REGINALD BLANCHARD
HOWARD BLOCK
RAY BONTE
ROBERT BRAUN
JEFF BROOKS
LARRY BRUCH
WILLIAM BURRELL
GHALIB CARMICHAEL
JOSEPH CATALANO
CHRIS CORNELL
JOHN CORREA
RALPH COSTANZA
MAUREEN CUMMINS
WILLIAM CUMMINS
RUSS DALTON
GAYLE DeGRACIA
NELSON DeGRACIA
NAZIF DERVISEVIC
DENNIS DIDIO
ARTHUR DRAGO
TOM DUJARDIN
DAWOOD EMMENUEL
JIM EVERY
DOUG FAIRCHILD
ERNIE FERRARA
ROY FINOCCHIO
SUZANNE FISCHER
JAMES FITZGERALD
KEITH FRANCO
SAL FRANCO, JR.
WILLIAM FRIESELL
JOE FUSCHI
STEVE GABRIEL
EDDIE GARCIA
HARRIS GLASSER
RAY GLYNN
MARK GOLDENBERG
FRANK GRANT
GEORGE GROSS
VITO GUARDIA
CHARLES GUSTAFI
ED HALL, JR.

SAPSANGA HALLIDAY
ROBERT HARRIS
JAY HAWKINS
GREG HELM
MONTAGUE HENRY
ZENKO HESHIKI
ROBERT HODES
ROY HOLMES
CHRIS HOWSMAN
GUS IMPAGLIAZZO
AL IRIZARY
JOHN JACKA
DOUG JACOBS
BOB JANTZEN
BILL JENSEN
JOE JOHNSON
KATHY KABBOORD
STEVE KABBOORD
MATT KAPLAN
JOSEPH KING
TONY LACAUZZI
STEVE LA NEGRO
NICK LECCESE
GEORGE LEE
RICHIE LEVITO
STEVE LOTT
RUDY LUNA
MICHAEL LUSHINGTON
TERRY MACCARRONE
JACK MACEDO
MICHAEL MACKAY
KIM MacMILLAN
JOE MALONE
MICHAEL MARGULIS
HENRY MARTIN
ANGELO MAZZA
HUGH McGOVERN
KATHY McMAHON
JOE McMAHON
PAUL MENARD
JIM MENDELSON
KEN MEYER
GREG MOLLER
JEFF MORIBER
ARTHUR NG
DAN NICHUALS
CHRIS NOTARILE
ANDREW OLSEN
MARIFE Y PALMA-GIL
SAM PALMER
G. MICHAEL PETERS
JOHN PEZZULLI
PRESTON POWELL II

RICHARD T. PULLEY
NICHOLAS RACANELLI
VICTOR RAMIREZ
EDDIE RAMOS
KEVIN L. REYMOND
DAVID RIEUMONT
MARK RIEUMONT
JOE ROBERTS
CLIFF ROMAIN
DONALD ROMARD
KIM ROSADO
MICHAEL ROSATI
KEN RUIZ
GREG RUSSELL
JOHN RUSSELL
JOYCE SANTAMARIA
WALT SAPRONOV
SERGE SAVITCHEFF
DION SCAGLIONE
JUDITH T. SCAGLIONE
ROBERT SCAGLIONE
ROBERT SCAGLIONE, JR.
SAL SCAGLIONE
JOSEPH SCHAUER
CECILE SCHOBERLE
CAROLL A. SCOFIELD
DAVE SEEGER
HOLLY WHITSTOCK SEEGER
SASHA SHAPIRO
ROB SMITH
PETER STAVRIDES
DAVID STENHOUSE
LOU SUFFREDINI
GARY TIKTIN
ROBERT TURNER
ANDO UESHIRO
ANGIRO UESHIRO
PETER VAN WESTERING
CHRISTINE WALKER
JAMES WAX
JOANNE WILLIAMSON
BOB YARNALL
RAY YAWORSKI
NIR ZAMIR
JOE ZEO
JAMES ZERMONO
ELLIOTT ZGODNY

Black Belts / *continued 1991 to 2010*

ADEL ABOUCHAEV
JOHN ADAMS
DALE ADAMSON
HEATHER ADAMSON
LORENZO AGUON
CARMELO ALEMAN
EDGAR AMROSIO
RON BALLIN
TZVI BAR-SHAI
CHRIS BARNES
DON BARNHART
PAM BEHRENS
JOEL BIERWERT
LOUANNE BIERWERT
GARY BIVONA
JONATHAN BLUM
JOHN BOTTEGA
DON BRACKEN
SHARON BRANT
VAL BROCHARD
JAMES BROOKS
KAREN BROPHY
JOSEPH BURNS
JENNIFER BURRILL
KATHERINE BURRILL
KEITH BURROWS
TOM BUTLER
RAFI CANETI
JEFF CANTOR
DAVID CARRIGAN
DES CHASKELSON
ELLIOT CLARK
MATHEW CODY
JONATHAN COHEN
PHIL COLLINS
PRICILLA DABBS-COOPER
SHLOMO DADON
JIM DAVIS
LUZ DELUCIA
ROBERT DOBROW
KRISTEN DOMINGER
LUKE DRAGAMONI
JOHN DRAGHI
ADAM DUNSBY
CARLA EDDY
HEND ELSAYED
KEITH ENG
MADELINE ESCOBAR
VERN FATH
MATTHEW FAULKNER
MOSTAPHA FAYE
FELIPE FLORES
MARAU GARAU
SCOTT GARLAND
KIM GARON
RICHY GLASSBERG
GERALDINE GLASSMAN
ROI GLOBEN
CHRISTOPHER GOBILLOT

CINDY GOBILLOT
DANIEL GOBILLOT
JEAN GOBILLOT
DEBY GOLDENBERG
STEFAN GRANT
BORIS GROSSMAN
JEFF GUCKER
EDYE HARKENRIDER
JEAN HARRIS
LEE-ANN HARTLEY
LISA HARVEY
PAZ HERSHKO
JOE HOPKINS
ROBIN ISLAM
ANIL JAISING
JOE JANSEN
D.J. JOHNSON
MICHAEL KARMODY
HOWARD KATALANSKI
DANIEL KAREN
SHABBIR KAZMI
LORI KLEIN
LYLE KLEUSCH
MICHAEL KLIEGMAN
JOSEPH KNIGHT
TERESA KNIGHT
WILLIAM KOLBERT
RICHARD KROMAR
MAX KUSHNER
YURI KUZNETSOV
ALAN LAI
EMMANUEL LAJUGIE-SAUJET
SCOTT LAWLOR
DANIEL LAX
JOHN L. LEE
KATHLEEN LEMIRE
LAWRENCE LINK III
RICHARD LOWE
JAMES LUNG
MICHAEL MA
RUILONG MA
TRACY MAGDALENE
AMY E. MAGER
PAT MARCHETTI
RON MARCHETTI
DERREK MARCUS
THOMAS MARCUS
HANNAH MARKOWITZ
JONAH MARKOWITZ
LISA MARKOWITZ
PATRICK R. MARKOWITZ
RAND MASON
EMILIANO MAZLEN
MATTHEW McHUGH
MARY McKITRICK
ROCHELLE MELTON
CHRIS MEMOLI
TYTUS MICHALSKI
GLENN MILLER

ANNA MILLER-HODES
SHACHAR MILLIS
KEREN MILLIS
ELLIN MOORE
PAT MORIARTY
JOE MOTRO
FRANK MOWKA
ROBERT NEFF
LEROY NUNERY
CHRISTINE O'HARA
KASHE OSCARSON
KENAR OSCARSON
KENNETH OSCARSON
NANCY OWEN
STEVEN PARSONS
CATHIE PARSONS
ERIK PASSOJA
SEAN PAUS
ASHOK PAWAR
HAVEN PELL
LYNN PELLAS
ELLIOT J. POTTER
IVAN PRYBYLO
SHLOMY QUARTLER
TOM QUINN
KRISTA RACHO-JANSEN
GAMIEL RAMSON
JOHN ROBBINS
TONY ROBINSON
KATHERINE ROCHE
CONNIE RUTKOWSKI
LOUIS RUVOLO
JOHN SACKREY
BILL SAFFRAN
SHANE SCAGLIONE
SHELLEY
   SCHLOSSBERG-GUCKER
MICHAEL SCOMILLIO
REBECCA SCOTT
JACK SELLATI
STAV SHAMIR
SIMEON SHARP
BRUCE SILVER
DAVID SILVERMAN
LORI SPIELBERGER-KLEIN
RICHARD STENHOUSE
DANIEL STOBOZKOI
NEIL TALBOT
DAVID TAMIR
KURT TEZEL
TREVOR TEZEL
MARK TONGRET
FRANK TORRES
LEN TRAN
RICHARD VACHINO
RICHARD WADDELL
HENRI WAELBROECK
DAN WEISS
STEPHEN WONG
JOE ZHANG
ERIC ZIMMERMAN
MATTHEW ZUCKER

ROBERT SCAGLIONE, Hanshi, began his karate training in 1967. This is his 40th anniversary as a Black belt under Grand Master Ansei Ueshiro, founder of the Shorin-ryu Karate USA system. Hanshi Scaglione is the chief administrator of the original style in the United States. He has traveled with Grand Master Ansei Ueshiro throughout the U.S.A. and as his representative worldwide. Born in Brooklyn, New York, Hanshi served in the U.S. Navy and became a NYC Police Officer. He voluntarily worked exclusively in high crime/high hazard areas during his entire 20 year tenure with the NYPD. He served in many assignments in all five boroughs of New York City including uniformed street cop, undercover officer and as a detective in the elite special investigation unit featured in the film "The French Connection."

He led the NYPD in felony arrests many times and has numerous awards, citations and letters of commendation from Police Department officials, Federal Agencies, District Attorneys, Grand Jurors and the civilian community. He retired from police service in order to devote himself full time to the art of karate.

Hanshi began his karate training in the NYPD. He continued his training under Sensei Terry Maccarrone, Shihan of the Hegashi Karate Dojo on Long Island, New York. He was Senior Instructor at the St. James Dojo for five years. Master Ueshiro, wanting a dojo in Manhattan, asked Hanshi to open a dojo in New York City. He founded the NYC dojo in 1977, which became the headquarters of the Shorin-Ryu Karate USA several years later. After ten years, in 1987, Hanshi relocated to Merritt Island, Florida and founded the Okinawan Karate Dojo leaving his senior student David Baker, San Dan to continue operation of the NYC Hombu dojo.

Over 250 students began their training directly under Hanshi Scaglione and have attained black belt level. He continues to work closely with all his black belts, including those who have opened the (18) dojo/clubs on the mainland US, Hawaii, China, and in Israel. Among his students are many professionals, doctors, lawyers, military officers, police officers, business executives, artists, writers, housewives, students and children.

Hanshi is the co-author with artist Bill Cummins, Ni Dan of "The Shorin-Ryu Karate Question and Answer Book" and has written another entitled "Building Warrior Spirit." His student David Seeger, Shichi Dan, an Emmy Award winner, has produced several karate videos with Hanshi. Hanshi has written and assisted his students in writing newspaper and magazine articles, film scripts on varied subjects, novels, and stage plays. He has appeared on national TV and radio, in stage productions, and at universities and schools giving karate demonstrations and lectures on self-defense and assault prevention. Hanshi has four sons. Sal is a Go Dan black belt, and Co-Shihan at the East Meets West Karate School of Northern Virginia. His sons Robert Jr., Dion and Shane are all Dan level black belts.

WILLIAM CUMMINS , was born in Santa Monica, California in 1929. He graduated from the High School of Industrial Art in 1948. After a four year stint in the army paratroopers during the Korean war, Sensei Cummins returned to his career as a painter. He was affiliated with the Brata Gallery, exhibiting his work during the heyday of the NY School of action painters. He has also exhibited at the Staten Island Museum and the Hudson River Museum.

He joined Person to Person Karate in 1979, and received his first degree blackbelt in 1982 at the age of fifty-two, proving that age is no barrier to success in karate training. He was promoted to second degree black belt in 1984. In addition to his martial arts studies, Sensei Cummins is an avid figure skater and flute player.

Both of Sensei Cummins' children have been involved in karate. His youngest daughter Maureen holds the rank of second degree black belt.